BR STEAM IN COLOUR

LONDON
TO ABERDEEN

Edinburgh Haymarket 60529

Peppercorn A2 Class Pacific locomotive no. 60529 *Pearl Diver* was built at Doncaster Works in February 1948. The locomotive was allocated to Edinburgh Haymarket shed for the majority of its career, and is pictured here on the Haymarket turntable. Its only other allocation was to St Margaret's shed from October 1961 until its withdrawal in December 1962. *Pearl Diver* is seen fitted with a M.L.S multi-valve regulator and a double chimney.

Aberdeen 60016

This photograph taken at Aberdeen Ferryhill Junction shows Class A4 4-6-2 locomotive no. 60016 *Silver King* south of the station and just north of Ferryhill engine shed. The junction signal box seen in the background was opened in 1905 and closed in 1981 when the system was upgraded. The engine emerged from Doncaster in November 1935 as part of the first four to be built. Originally the locomotive would have been fitted with a Flamen speed recorder, which transferred the speed of the locomotive to apparatus inside the cab. These were later abandoned and in the late 1950s Smith-Stone speed indicators were fitted to the left-hand-side rear crank pin, as seen here. *Silver King* had the apparatus added at Doncaster during a general repair between May and July 1960. The locomotive was withdrawn from Aberdeen in March 1965.

BR STEAM IN COLOUR

LONDON TO ABERDEEN

FROM THE BILL REED COLLECTION

PETER TUFFREY

FONTHILL

Dundee West 62485

Built as part of NBR Class K at Cowlairs Works in April 1919, 4-4-0 locomotive no. 62485 *Glen Murran* became part of LNER Class D34 at Grouping. The engine is seen in the old Dundee West shed yard, which was utilised by Dundee Tay Bridge shed as a storage area when the former closed in 1951. Dundee West had been opened by the Caledonian Railway in 1885 and was a large shed consisting of eight roads open at each end. It was refurbished in the late 1950s and by the early 1960s it housed a DMU maintenance depot. It closed in the 1980s and subsequently the site was cleared. No. 62485 was withdrawn from Dunfermline shed during March 1960.

First published 2013

Fonthill Media Limited
www.fonthillmedia.com
enquiries@fonthillmedia.com

Copyright © Peter Tuffrey 2013

The right of Peter Tuffrey to be identified as the Author
of this work has been asserted in accordance with the
Copyrights, Designs and Patents Act 1988.

British Library Cataloguing in Publication Data.
A catalogue record for this book is available from the British Library.

ISBN 978-1-78155-067-0

Typesetting and Origination by Fonthill Media.
Printed in Great Britain.

Contents

Acknowledgements

I would like to thank the following people for their help: Catherine at Book Law, Nottingham, Bill Hudson, Hugh Parkin, Bill Reed and Alan Sutton.

Special thanks are due to my son Tristram Tuffrey for his help throughout the course of the project.

I have taken reasonable steps to verify the accuracy of the information in this book but it may contain errors or omissions. Any information that may be of assistance to rectify any problems will be gratefully received. Please contact me by email: petertuffrey@rocketmail. com, or in writing: Peter Tuffrey, 8 Wrightson Avenue, Warmsworth, Doncaster, South Yorkshire, DN4 9QL.

Aberdeen Kittybrewster 64560
Pictured minus coupling rods at Kittybrewster shed is Class J37 0-6-0 locomotive no. 64560. The engine had two inside cylinders measuring 19½x26 inches and a Stephenson valve gear with piston valves measuring 9½ inches. Kittybrewster's first shed was built by the Great North of Scotland Railway in 1854. The building was a four-track straight shed situated on the west side of Kittybrewster Station. Construction of no. 64560 took place at the North British Locomotive Co.'s Atlas Works in July 1918. Its career had lasted almost forty-three years when it was withdrawn in March 1961.

Introduction

The pictures in this book were chosen from the many hundreds of 35-mm colour slides taken by Bill Reed on and off the route stretching from London to Aberdeen. Station scenes, views on works and in sheds are featured. They roughly cover a period from 1951 to 1967 and depict the last gasp of steam before the introduction of diesels, though a handful of early 'green' diesels are included. As if on some imaginary journey, the book begins at King's Cross Station, it wanders over to Liverpool Street, steps into Great Eastern country, and then meanders on and off the East Coast Main Line to finish at Aberdeen.

Bill Reed was born in Nottingham in 1933 and during his younger days, his mother frequently took him to visit her sister in Hucknall, Nottingham, travelling from Bullwell on the Sentinel Steam Railcars no. 5192 *Rising Sun* and no. 51908 *Expedition*. Yet, he has been told that even before then his paternal grandfather took him to watch trains at Bulwell Common. His grandfather was a retired driver, formerly on the MS&LR at Northwich. He came to Annesley, near Nottingham, to work on the GCR when it opened. Bill's father was also interested in transport, having been apprenticed at Broughs, the Bulwell motorcycle builders, and after the Second World War he worked at Wrigley's Wagon Repair Works in Nottingham. He also had an allotment, conveniently situated at the side of the Great Central line, overlooking Bulwell Common Sidings. To Bill it was a trainspotter's paradise, and he bought his first stock book, *Ian Allen's ABC of British Locomotives*, in 1943.

When Bill left school, he became a messenger lad at Nottingham Victoria Station enquiry office. Bill spent his lunch hours on the station platforms, where he first met Freddie Guildford, a well-known local railway enthusiast. In time he encouraged Bill to take photographs, develop films and make contact prints.

In 1950 Bill obtained a job as an engine cleaner, the first step in the long slow haul to becoming a driver. The progress was interrupted by National Service but he joined the RAF photographic club and was a member long enough to learn how to enlarge and print photographs.

Once demobbed, Bill bought an Agfa Super Isolette, which in 1955 was considered a very good camera. Bill returned to work at British Rail as a fireman on steam engines, including 4Fs, 8Fs and Class 5s. In 1966 he was passed for driving, but had to wait thirteen years before being made a regular driver. Unfortunately, by that time, steam had long since given way to diesel.

Throughout his life Bill has always taken black and white photographs, colour slides and also cine film of railways in this country, Eastern and Western Europe and in America. Bill used a

Mamiya 330 for most of his black and white photography, but he also used 35-mm Practicas, a Canon for colour, and a Bolex 8-mm cine.

Many of the pictures reproduced here were taken by Bill after work at weekends or during annual holidays. Frequently using his rail passes, taking advantage of organised 'railway trips' or riding as a passenger on a friend's motorbike he would find interesting locations where steam locomotives were still operating. It is amazing now to look at some of his pictures and realise that he was standing on railway track when he took them, unhindered by authority, yet always behaving responsibly. His closeness to his subjects is breathtaking at times, as many of the pictures in this book demonstrate.

This was a time when train spotting and taking pictures of steam locomotives was a revered pastime and not looked upon with derision and ridiculed as it is today. It was only natural for young lads to have a desire to look at the vast, almost human engines with awe, because maybe their dads, granddads or even great granddads had been part of building or working them. For decades the railways had touched the lives of many families across the entire country.

It is noticeable that Bill has depicted marvellously the post-Second World War atmosphere on the railways when steam was on its last legs; the vast majority of the locomotives are in a very grimy condition and a number are seen on the scrap line. There is also evidence, in the vast coal hoppers and water tanks for example, of how complicated and labour intensive it was to run a steam engine. How curious it must have been for loco drivers and firemen to move from the rigours of firing and raising steam on a steam loco to stepping inside the cab of a diesel and pressing a button to make it work.

Many of the well-known sheds where vast numbers of locomotives were allocated were a source of much inspiration for Bill. For example he was very active shooting film at Grantham, Doncaster, York, Darlington, Edinburgh Haymarket, Dundee and Aberdeen, and at times it was very difficult to know what to include and to leave out of this book. I have noted in the text the history of many of these sheds and, where appropriate, their status today. A selection of the pictures that Bill Reed took around Nottingham formed the basis of an earlier book *The Last Days of Steam in Nottinghamshire from the Bill Reed Collection*, published by Alan Sutton in 2010. Another one, entitled *Working and Preserved Industrial Locomotives from the Bill Reed Collection* appeared in 2012 with Alan Sutton's Fonthill Media.

When steam workings were restricted in England during the early 1960s, Bill trekked with a friend, most notably Don Beecroft, to Scotland. In many instances they found places of interest where there were not only A4s and A1s, but operational locomotives with a longer history. Many are featured in the sections over the border. But what is remarkable about this book is the vast number of locomotive classes included in the British and Scottish sections. The task of documenting them was enormous as the long bibliography at the back testifies.

The new 'green' diesels shown here look remarkably modern and more efficient than their steam counterparts, and that is why they have been included – as a stark contrast to their predecessors. But many of them have in turn given way to electrics in the intervening years.

Looking back now at the 1950s and 1960s, Bill says he would have taken many more pictures of steam locomotives in their final years. But that is no matter, he has taken enough to give us more than a hint of what it was like in the last days of steam on and off the East Coast route.

CHAPTER 1

London King's Cross to Peterborough

London King's Cross 60131

Peppercorn A1 Class 4-6-2 locomotive no. 60131 *Osprey* is photographed leaving Platform 8 (now 7) at King's Cross Station. Behind the locomotive, the top of King's Cross signal box can be seen; it was located at the end of Platforms 5 and 6 (now 4 and 5). The signalling was upgraded to electrified colour signals during the 1930s and the signal box was demolished around 1976. *Osprey* was built at Darlington in October 1948 and allocated to King's Cross from new. Moves to Grantham and Copley Hill followed, and from the latter it would have worked services including the Yorkshire Pullman, Queen of Scots Pullman and Harrogate Sunday Pullman. *Osprey* had two further moves to Ardsley and Neville Hill in the early 1960s before withdrawal came in October 1965.

London Liverpool Street 61607

Locomotive no. 61607 *Blickling*, seen at Liverpool Street Station turntable, was one of the first ten Gresley B17 4-6-0 Class to be ordered from the North British Locomotive Co. during December 1928. These locomotives were prone to cracked frames; it was decided to replace the frames on nine of the ten. No. 61607 (as LNER 2807) was in works from the end of December 1931 to July 1932 having the problem corrected. *Blickling* was rebuilt by Thompson to B2 Class at Darlington in May 1947, becoming LNER no. 1607 before receiving its BR number in June 1949. It is shown with a NER-type tender from a C7 Atlantic, installed during the rebuilding, which had a larger capacity than its original GER-type tender. No. 61607 was the last of the B2s to be withdrawn in December 1959.

London Liverpool Street Station 70010

British Railways Standard Class 7 4-6-2 locomotive no. 70010 *Owen Glendower,* built at Crewe Works in May 1951, initially operated from Norwich shed. In the background on the right, the cab approach road from Pindar Street provides a good vantage point for two young boys who were no doubt fascinated by the workings at the station. No. 70010 *Owen Glendower* is named after the fourteenth-century Prince of Wales and character in Shakespeare's *Henry IV Part 1*. No. 70010 was at Norwich shed for just over ten years before moving to March shed in 1961 and then Willesden in 1963. This was followed by a succession of moves in 1965 to Crewe North, Crewe South and Carlisle Kingmoor where the engine was removed from service in September 1967.

London Liverpool Street 69677

The Broadgate development is now situated above this part of Liverpool Street Station. Class N7/2 0-6-2T locomotive no. 69677, built at Gorton Works in December 1927, featured a Belpaire firebox, increased valve travel and maximum cut-off. The locomotive was later rebuilt with a round-top firebox in November 1946, becoming N7/3. The engine is seen with a high-sided bunker, while a number of other members of the class had coal rails. No. 69677 was withdrawn in November 1960.

London Liverpool Street 61976

Gresley Class K3 2-6-0 locomotive entered traffic from Darlington in November 1936. A total of 193 engines were built between 1920 and 1937 in four works – Doncaster, Darlington, Armstrong Whitworth and Robert Stephenson & Co. The locomotive was among the final batch of twenty K3s built at Darlington. No. 61976 has the group standard tender that had a capacity of 4,200 gallons of water and over 7 tons of coal. It has straight sides and vacuum brakes with the vacuum reservoir visible at the rear of the tender. No. 61976 was withdrawn in January 1962.

London Liverpool Street 70011

British Railways Standard Class 7 4-6-2 locomotive no. 70011 *Hotspur* emerged from Crewe Works in May 1951. It was a member of the Britannia Class and built to the designs of R. Riddles. In *British Railways Standard Steam Locomotives Volume 1* by the Railway Correspondence and Travel Society, the cost of the first ten engines is given as £20,114, but for the last one the cost had risen closer to £24,000. This was due to the fitting of different components to the later engines, such as ATC apparatus and different axle bearings. A total of fifty-five locomotives were built, all at Crewe. No. 70011 is photographed approaching Liverpool Street Station; it was withdrawn in December 1967 and scrapped.

London Liverpool Street 69614

Liverpool Street Station was opened in February 1874 by the Great Eastern Railway as the London terminus for their lines from the east. The station replaced an old terminus at Bishopsgate, built in 1840, which became a goods depot in the early 1880s and remained active until the 1960s. N7 Class 0-6-2T locomotive no. 69614 entered traffic from Stratford Works in December 1923. Despite being built after Grouping, the locomotive still followed the design of A. J. Hill's Great Eastern Railway Class L77; later engines were modified by the LNER. No. 69614 became the Liverpool Street west side pilot engine in 1956 so its appearance always had to be in good condition, as seen here, with polished metalwork and bright paintwork. In time it lost the duty to a diesel locomotive and was withdrawn in December 1960.

London Liverpool Street 61629

Gresley B17 4-6-0 locomotive no. 61629 *Naworth Castle* was erected at Darlington Works in April 1931. Seventy-three of the class were built; the first ten at North British Locomotive Co., fifty-two at Darlington and eleven at Robert Stephenson & Co. No. 61629 fell into Class B17/2 as it had slight modifications from those classed B17/1, which were the ten built at NBLC. The class was rebuilt with different boilers from the 1940s, however, no. 61629 was one of six to retain the original type boiler throughout its working life. September 1959 was the month that *Naworth Castle* left service and it was subsequently scrapped.

London Liverpool Street 70036

Liverpool Street Station was designed by E. Wilson on the site which had previously been occupied by the Bethlem Royal Hospital. In the 1980s and the early 1990s the station was redeveloped although some of the original features remain. British Railways Standard Class 7, 4-6-2 locomotive no. 70036 *Boadicea*, is reversing into one of the platforms. The engine was erected at Crewe Works in December 1952, entering service towards the end of the month to Stratford shed. From there, the locomotive worked east from Liverpool Street Station to Norwich and Ipswich on both passenger and freight services. No. 70036 was allocated to Norwich from February 1959 to October 1960 and would have operated similar services from that location. The locomotive was withdrawn from Carlisle Kingmoor shed in October 1966.

Stratford Shed 65445

Class J15 0-6-0 locomotive no. 65445 is pictured at Stratford shed. The engine was built at Stratford Works during August 1899 for the GER to the designs of T. W. Worsdell's Class Y14. In total, 289 engines were built between 1883 and 1913; 272 were still in operation at the time of Grouping. This had dropped considerably to 127 at the formation of BR. No. 65445 is looking the worse for wear and lacking a boiler dome. The engine was allocated to Colchester at the time of the picture, leaving for Parkeston Quay in November 1959 before final allocation at Stratford in January 1961. No. 65445 was withdrawn in August 1962.

Stratford Works Departmental 33

GER Class B74 0-4-0T locomotive no. 210 was built at Stratford Works in January 1921. The locomotive was immediately placed in service stock, operating throughout its life on shunting duties in Stratford Works yard. The engine was designed by A. J. Hill and became part of LNER Class Y4 (no. 7210) at Grouping. The locomotives were powerful for their size and employed where larger engines could not work. No. 7210 carried BR no. 68129 from October 1948 until renumbered Departmental 33 in September 1953. The locomotive was withdrawn ten years later in December 1963 and scrapped on site.

Stratford Shed 70000

British Railways Standard Class 7 4-6-2 locomotive no. 70000 *Britannia* entered traffic from Crewe Works in January 1951. The engine is pictured at Stratford shed with the mechanical coaling plant visible in the background. The coaling plant was unlike others seen around the country as it had a larger capacity and was able to dispense coal to more engines. Built in 1922 the facility had a capacity of 800 tons and could refuel seven locomotives at once. It has since been demolished and the site is now part of Stratford International Station. *Britannia* was withdrawn in May 1966 and went into preservation; it is currently owned by Royal Scot Locomotive and General Trust Ltd.

Stratford 70035

Stratford Works was constructed by the Eastern Counties Railway in 1847 and was manufacturing locomotives by 1850. The works passed into the hands of the GER when the ECR was absorbed in 1862, becoming the former's principle locomotive builder. The works stopped producing engines and became responsible for maintenance and repair when absorbed by the LNER in 1924. British Railways Standard Class 7 no. 70035 *Rudyard Kipling* emerged from Crewe Works in December 1952. The locomotive has the standard Brunswick green livery lined with black and orange. On the tender is the later BR emblem. The locomotive carried tender no. 854 when new, which had a capacity of 4,250 gallons of water and 7 tons of coal. The locomotive was one of eight in the class to be withdrawn at the end of December 1967.

Stratford Shed 69709

Class N7/3 0-6-2T locomotive no. 69709 was built at Doncaster in December 1927. Thirty-three N7s were built there between 1927 and 1928. There were slight differences in these engines from those built earlier, the main one being the change of boiler to a round-top design. The locomotive went to Stratford shed from new to work the London suburban services. Moves to Hatfield and Colchester came in the 1950s before returning to Stratford in October 1957. No. 69709 left service in November 1960, a casualty of the emerging diesels and electrics.

Stratford 64666

At the Stratford shed ash pits is Class J19 0-6-0 locomotive no. 64666. The engine was built for the GER at Stratford Works in November 1918 as part of the T77 Class. The latter were a modified version of the GER Class E72 locomotives, both designed by A. J. Hill. Twenty-five T77 locomotives had been built at Grouping and were then classified J19 by the LNER. In the mid-1930s, the company began to rebuild the class; no. 64666 (LNER no. 8266) was modified in August 1936. This work included replacing the Belpaire firebox with a round top version, increasing the diameter of the boiler and replacing the cab. January 1961 witnessed the locomotive's withdrawal from Stratford.

Stratford Shed D5542

Stratford Works continued to maintain steam locomotives until 1962 when reorganisation saw the closure of much of the site. Part of it was retained and rededicated to the maintenance of diesel locomotives, which ceased in 1991. The British Railways Class 31 A1A-A1A diesel locomotives, also known as the Brush Type 2 and originally as Class 30, were built by Brush Traction, Loughborough, from 1957-62. The locomotive here emerged from Loughborough in July 1959, and is photographed adjacent to the Stratford engine repair shop. The fleet of locomotives were originally built with Mirrlees engines, but these proved to be unsuccessful and were replaced by English Electric Co. units. D5542 received one in August 1968 and was subsequently reclassified as Class 31. At the TOPS renumbering, the locomotive became 31 124, and it carried this number from January 1973 until it was withdrawn in May 1990 and scrapped.

Stratford 69715

Class N7 0-6-2T locomotive no. 69715 entered traffic from Doncaster Works in January 1928 in class part three. Engines in this part of the class were also built with round-top boilers. No. 69715 had Westinghouse and vacuum brakes fitted when new; these were used throughout its time in service. The water tank had a capacity of 1,600 gallons and the coal bunker could hold over 3 tons of coal. The tank is seen with the second BR emblem, which is applied the wrong way round. Withdrawal came for the locomotive in December 1960.

Stratford D226

English Electric Prototype 0-6-0 diesel shunting locomotive no. D226 was built at Vulcan Foundry, Newton-le-Willows, in 1956. The locomotive was one of only two made by English Electric as a demonstration locomotive to British Railways who assessed the locomotives at Stratford Works. Both prototypes were built with 500-hp engines but they differed as D226 was diesel-electric while its sister engine D227 was diesel-hydraulic. D226 was renumbered in August 1959 to D0226 to allow a British Railways Class 40 diesel locomotive to take over the number. D0226 was removed from service in October 1960 and has since gone into preservation at the Keighley & Worth Valley Railway. D0227 was scrapped. Seen to the right is British Railways Class 08 0-6-0 shunting engine no. D3683, built at Doncaster Works in 1958 and a long-time Stratford resident before withdrawal in 1993.

Stratford 61644

Class B17 4-6-0 locomotive no. 61644 *Earlham Hall* was erected at Darlington Works in May 1935. It was one of five engines built in class part three, which had GER-type tenders and modifications made to the frames. In March 1949 the locomotive was rebuilt as a Thompson B2 at Darlington. Along with the other alterations made to no. 61644, Westinghouse brakes were fitted in addition to the original vacuum brakes. *Earlham Hall* left service from Cambridge in November 1959 after a three-year allocation.

Stratford Shed 61608

Gresley B17 Class 4-6-0 locomotive no. 61608 *Gunton*, pictured at Stratford shed, was built at N.B. Locomotive Co. in December 1928. After running in around Scotland the locomotive was allocated to Stratford, where four of the first ten in the class found themselves. By 1935 the B17 allocation had risen to fourteen with one addition before the Second World War. Upon Nationalisation, the class had become more dispersed and Stratford's allocation had dropped to six, but it had risen again by 1951 to eighteen. No. 61608 was a long-term Stratford resident; it is seen outside the shed building undergoing some maintenance. It is attached to a GER-type tender that held 3,700 gallons of water and 4 tons of coal. It has the later BR emblem, which is the wrong way round. The locomotive was withdrawn from Cambridge shed in March 1960.

Stratford Shed 61658

Pictured at Stratford shed, no. 61658 *The Essex Regiment* emerged from Darlington Works in May 1936 as *Newcastle United*, but was renamed the following month. As LNER no. 2858, the locomotive was coupled to a group standard tender with a higher capacity and straight sides. When the locomotive was renamed, it was also decided to switch the tender with no. 2847 *Helmingham Hall*. No. 61658 is shown with a GER type tender with vacuum brakes; the reservoir cylinder is clearly visible at the rear. Only four other engines with GER tenders had vacuum brakes. The locomotive was withdrawn in December 1959.

Stratford D8402

British Railways Class 16 diesel Bo-Bo locomotive D8402 entered traffic from the North British Locomotive Co., Queens Park Works, in June 1958. Ten of the locomotives were built as a test batch and evaluated against similar engines but no more were produced as they were found to be prone to engine problems. They were all allocated to Stratford where they were used for freight services. D8402 is seen in the yard next to Class 24 no. D5031. The Class 16 locomotives were withdrawn in 1968, D8402 going in July. All of the class were scrapped.

Stratford D5031

Class 24 diesel-electric locomotive no. D5031, pictured at Stratford, was built at Crewe Works in June 1959 to a design which originated from Derby Works as part of the Pilot Scheme. Between 1958 and 1961, Derby, Crewe and Darlington Works produced 151 of the class. The locomotives were fitted with Sulzer 6LDA28 diesel engines and British Thomson-Houston generators. D5031 was allocated to March when new, moving to Stratford two months later, then to Willesden in January 1961. As no. 24 031, the engine was withdrawn in October 1975 and scrapped at Swindon. The last of the class, no. 24 081, left service in 1980 and was preserved along with three others.

Cambridge 70039

Cambridge Railway Station was opened in 1845 by the Eastern Counties Railway, with alterations occurring during 1863 and 1908. British Railways Standard Class 7 4-6-2 locomotive no. 70039 *Sir Christopher Wren* was built at Crewe Works in February 1953 and allocated to Norwich. Four months later it was at Stratford, where it was resident for six years before returning to Norwich. Moves to Immingham, Carlisle Upperby and Carlisle Kingmoor followed in the 1960s. From Immingham the locomotive worked the Grimsby to King's Cross service and was also employed on express fish trains. Withdrawal came in September 1967.

Cambridge 62035

Peppercorn Class K1 2-6-0 locomotive no. 62035 is seen waiting at Cambridge South signal box, which was located at the southern end of the station. The engine emerged from N.B. Locomotive Co., Queens Park Works, in September 1949 and was allocated to March shed. This latter was utilised for many K1s, housing thirty of the seventy locomotives in 1950. No. 62035 moved to Frodingham in December 1960 where a number of other K1s were to be found. Their duties included handling the heavy trains bound for the steelworks nearby. No. 62035 was withdrawn in July 1965.

Cambridge 65520

0-6-0 locomotive no. 65520, (ex-GER Class F48 no. 1170, and later Class J17 LNER no. 8170) was built at Stratford Works during September 1901, the first of ten to be erected there in September and October of that year. The locomotive was designed by J. Holden. In subsequent years, the engines were rebuilt with Belpaire fireboxes and some were superheated by both the GER and LNER. No. 1170 was rebuilt by the GER in December 1921. The locomotive was allocated to Cambridge for seven years from March 1954 until withdrawal in February 1961.

Cambridge 68609

This Class J69/1 0-6-0T locomotive, built at Stratford Works in June 1901 as GER Class R24, was designed by J. Holden. One hundred and forty locomotives were built to the design, which was based on the GER T18 Class, for shunting and passenger services. Due to a change in GER requirements, ninety-five of the class were rebuilt with new, more powerful boilers and larger tanks. No. 68609 was altered in August 1915. It was subsequently refitted with a smaller boiler by the LNER in September 1938 when it was reclassified J67/2. A further boiler change occurred in June 1952 when it again received the larger boiler and was reclassified again to J69/1. The locomotive is pictured in a run-down state at Cambridge GER shed. The mechanical coaler seen in the background was added in 1932. The locomotive was withdrawn in September 1962.

Cambridge 43155

The LMS Ivatt Class 4 2-6-0 locomotive was introduced in 1947, one of only three being built before Nationalisation, out of an eventual total of 162. They were classified 4MT by BR and building was completed by 1952. No. 43155, erected at Doncaster Works in December 1951, was allocated to Melton Constable when entering service. The engine had a brief stay at Boston before an allocation to Colwick, where it spent the latter part of its career. Withdrawal came in January 1965.

Cambridge 64654

The GER shed at Cambridge was located at the north end of the station on the west side of the lines. Three locomotive sheds were employed at Cambridge: the Eastern Counties Railway (1847), Bedford and Cambridge Railway (1862) and the Great Northern Railway (1869). The ECR shed, which became the GER shed, was originally a four-road dead-end structure. In 1913 it was extended to seven roads and it was further enlarged in 1931. By this date the other companies' sheds had closed and the GER one became the main shed. It closed to steam in June 1962 and was demolished in 1964 to accommodate a car park. Class J19 0-6-0 locomotive no. 64654, built at Stratford Works in October 1916 as GER Class T77, was photographed outside the GER shed and removed from service in January 1960.

Cambridge 61568

GER Class S69 4-6-0 locomotive no. 1568 was built in June 1920 at Stratford Works. Seventy locomotives were erected by the GER to the design of S. D. Holden, with the LNER producing ten during 1928. At Grouping the LNER reclassified the locomotives as B12 and no. 1568 was renumbered 8568. It received the number 7482 in October 1942, changing again in September 1946 to 1568 and acquiring its BR number in October 1948. The locomotive was rebuilt in April 1941 and reclassified B12/3. Changes to the design included a new boiler, front end and valve gear. The engine was allocated to Norwich Thorpe shed at the time of the photograph and it was withdrawn from there after a five-year allocation in August 1959.

March Shed 62070

Peppercorn Class K1 2-6-0 locomotive no. 62070, the last of the class to be built at North British Locomotive Co., entered service in March 1950. The K1s were a modification of the Thompson K1/1 locomotive, which was rebuilt from a Gresley Class K4 engine. Peppercorn altered the running plate, pony truck springs, boiler roof stays and smokebox door. The Peppercorn K1s also had an increased capacity tender from the 3,500 gallons and over 5 tons of coal capacity of the K1/1 to 4,200 gallons and over 7 tons of coal. The locomotive was withdrawn along with a number of other K1s in January 1965.

March Shed 64774

Two hundred and eighty-nine locomotives were built to the Class J39 0-6-0 design and they worked on freight services and occasionally passenger trains. No. 64774 entered traffic from Darlington Works in March 1929 and its first allocation was to York shed. It is seen with a group standard tender, which held 3,500 gallons of water and 5½ tons of coal. The locomotive was allocated to March shed in the twilight of its career, arriving in March 1958. It was withdrawn from there in March 1960 and was scrapped at Stratford.

March Shed 62618

Designed by A. J. Hill, Class D16 4-4-0 no. 62618 locomotive entered traffic from Stratford Works in August 1923. The engine was originally classified H88 by the GER and was one of ten built. The design was based on earlier GER Classes S46 and D56, the difference being the increased size of the boiler the addition of a Belpaire firebox and superheater. The LNER increased the size of the smokebox of the D16s (reclassified from H88) in the late 1920s, with no. 62618 (as LNER no. 8787) changing in January 1929, being reclassified D16/2. The engine was later rebuilt with a new boiler, slightly modified from the original, with a round-top firebox to become D16/3. The engine retained its slide valves and valances over the wheels, which some rebuilds had lost due to other modifications. No. 62618 was withdrawn from March shed in November 1959.

March Shed 63747

The mechanical coaler at March shed was installed around 1923 by the Mitchell Conveyor & Transporter Company. Seen in front of it is Class 04 2-8-0 locomotive, no. 63747 built in November 1917 at the North British Locomotive Company's Queens Park Works. Based on GCR Class 8K by J. Robinson, the locomotives were used for heavy goods trains. The design was adopted during the First World War by the Railway Operating Division for use on the continent, and a total of 521 locomotives were built, including no. 63747 (as ROD no. 1824). Only minor modifications were made, including the use of steel plate for the firebox instead of copper, which was in short supply. The locomotive was one of 100 bought by the LNER in 1927 from the ROD and it entered service in May. Its career lasted a further thirty-four years before withdrawal came in May 1961.

March Shed 60803

The original shed at March was built by the ECR in 1850. It was replaced by a structure erected by the GER in 1884, consisting of six tracks. After Grouping the LNER added a four-track shed and in the early 1930s it added a five-track washout shed. The shed closed to steam at the end of 1963 and became a home for diesel locomotives. Gresley's Class V2 2-6-2 locomotive no. 60803, was in the initial group of five built at Doncaster, emerging from there in October 1936. The locomotive was allocated to Peterborough New England when new, working on the Glasgow goods service and weekend passenger services. It had a long stay at March shed from July 1953 to November 1961 when it returned to New England. It was withdrawn from there in June 1963.

March Shed 63924

Gresley Class 02 2-8-0 locomotive no. 62924 was built at North British Locomotive Co., Atlas Works, during May 1921 for the Great Northern Railway. Eleven of the locomotives were built for the GNR, with the LNER building fifty-six, the last one appearing in 1943. No. 63924 is photographed with unlined black livery, which the class had applied under the supervision of BR. The locomotive is attached to a GNR-type tender with a capacity for 3,500 gallons of water and 6½ tons of coal. The cab is converted to the side window variety, which was altered in July 1939. No. 63924 left service in November 1963.

March Shed 61616

Thompson Class B2 4-6-0 locomotive no. 61616 *Fallodon* was originally built as Gresley Class B17, LNER no. 2816, at Darlington Works in October 1930. The engine was rebuilt as part of Thompson's standardisation plans in November 1945 at Darlington. The number of cylinders was reduced to two outside with an increase in the size of the piston valves to 10 inches. The boiler was diagram 100A and pressure was increased to 225 lbs. The front bogie was also repositioned. The locomotive was allocated to Clacton in the late 1940s, along with other B2s working to Liverpool Street Station. In 1954 it was reallocated to Colchester where it was put on services to London and Ipswich. Final allocation to Cambridge came in late 1956, and the locomotive was withdrawn in September 1959.

March Shed 65420

Class J15 0-6-0 locomotive no. 65420, built at Stratford Works in January 1892, incorporated a slightly modified design to those in the class built earlier. The main difference was that the engines built since 1891 had a sloping grate whereas the pre-1891 locomotives had level grates. Also, the later engines featured an altered valve gear and slightly larger wheel tyres. No. 65420 enjoyed an impressive seventy-year career before it was retired in August 1962.

March Shed 11101

Pictured at March shed, Class 04 0-6-0 diesel shunting engine was built at Vulcan Foundry for the Drewry Car Company Ltd in June 1952. The engine is seen with side skirting and cowcatchers, features only installed on the first four engines as they were intended to work on the public tramway systems at Wisbech and Yarmouth. No. 11101 was at Yarmouth South Town for two months between June and August 1952 before moving to March. Apart from a month at Plaistow in March 1955, no. 11101 was at March for fourteen years. During this time it received the pre-TOPS number D2201 in February 1962. The engine moved to Crewe before being withdrawn in April 1968.

March Shed 61610

B17 4-6-0 locomotive no. 61610 *Honingham Hall* was erected at Darlington Works in August 1930. It is pictured at the east side of March shed with a GER-type tender that has the later BR emblem, which is applied the wrong way round. When new the tender attached to no. 61610 was the first to carry the GNR-type axle boxes. This pattern was subsequently fitted to the proceeding members of the class and the preceding locomotives were also modified. The locomotive was rebuilt to B17 Class part 6 in October 1953 and was withdrawn in January 1960 from Cambridge Shed. It was allocated to March shed between April 1958 and December 1959.

March Shed 61633

Gresley Class B17 4-6-0 no. 61633 *Kimbolton Castle* is named after the former residence of the Duke of Manchester, located in Cambridgeshire. The house was sold in 1950 and is now occupied by a school. The engine entered service from Darlington in May 1931 in the second part of the class. In August 1948 the locomotive was fitted with a diagram 100A boiler, which was slightly different to the original diagram 100, having the boiler pressure increased 25lbs to 225psi. This alteration placed the locomotive in class part six. The locomotive left service in September 1959.

March Shed 62016

Peppercorn Class K1 2-6-0 locomotive no. 62016 was photographed at March shed looking like it had been hard at work. It was allocated to the shed for a large proportion of its career, spending just over ten years operating from there. Built by the NBLC's Queens Park Works in July 1949, the locomotive started its career at Gorton, arriving at March in May 1950. It left for Frodingham in December 1960 and was withdrawn from there in July 1963. The K1's duties from March shed included light goods and coal services to Temple Mills in London and East Anglia and also on some passenger services.

Peterborough New England 60513

Thompson Class A2/3 4-6-2 locomotive no. 60513 *Dante* entered traffic from Doncaster Works in August 1946. The design for this locomotive class was based on the A2/2 engines that were rebuilt by Thompson from the Gresley P2 Class. No. 60513 is photographed at the south end of New England shed, Peterborough, with the water gantry seen above the locomotive. Water at the shed was originally drawn from the River Nene and was later augmented by supplies from Peterborough Corporation Waterworks. However, these proved to be of poor quality and a solution came from boreholes at Werrington, which provided more than enough for the shed's needs. From New England, *Dante* worked main line passenger services and was withdrawn from there in April 1963.

Peterborough New England 15004

Class DES2 0-6-0 diesel-electric shunting locomotive, seen here at New England shed, was the only one of its type built. Construction work was carried out jointly by Doncaster Works, which produced the frames and body, and Brush Traction, which produced the engine and electrical components. The work was completed in November 1947 when the engine underwent performance testing at Stratford. It did not enter BR stock until April 1949. It carried the no. 15004 from May (the locomotive never carried its LNER no. 8004) and was later reclassified by BR to DEJ2. No. 15004 was allocated to New England in 1957 and spent the rest of its career at the shed, being withdrawn in October 1962 and scrapped at Doncaster.

Peterborough New England 60862

New England shed was always well stocked with Gresley Class V2 2-6-2 engines to work both passenger and goods services between London and York. No. 60862, built at Darlington Works in June 1939, is equipped with separate cylinders, which were fitted in March 1959. It has yet to receive a double chimney that was acquired in October 1961. The locomotive is seen at the south end of the engine shed with the fitting shop and wagon repair shop seen to the right of the engine. Withdrawal from service for no. 60862 came in June 1963.

Peterborough New England 60504

New England shed was built by the GNR in 1851 with six roads open at each end. In 1854 it was extended by a road at each end and again in 1866. Also, in the same year, the Peterborough Works tender and paint shops were utilised as engine sheds, increasing the covered space available. No further significant alterations to these structures occurred for the next 100 years. The site was cleared in 1969 after closure in September 1968. Thompson Class A2/2 4-6-2 locomotive no. 60504 *Mons Meg* was a rebuilt Gresley Class P2 2-8-2 engine. It was originally erected at Doncaster Works in July 1936 and rebuilding occurred in November 1944. *Mons Meg* is seen here in front of the locomotive shed at New England; it was withdrawn from there in January 1961.

Peterborough New England 64223
The locomotive is pictured in front of the old coal stage at New England shed, with its replacement, the mechanical coal stage, visible above the roof. The coal stage was constructed in 1905 to replace the original coal stage, erected in 1852, and a temporary coaling facility built in 1901. The mechanical coal stage was installed in 1930 and had a 500-ton capacity. The 1905 coal stage was retained for use at busy periods. Class J6 0-6-0 locomotive no. 64223 was built at Doncaster Works in October 1913. Designed by H. A. Ivatt for the GNR, the class was later modified by Gresley. A total of 110 engines were built for the GNR, who classified them J22. No. 64223 is seen here with a short chimney and small dome. Withdrawal came in April 1961.

CHAPTER 2

Grantham to Doncaster

Grantham 60065

Gresley Class A1 4-6-2 locomotive no. 60065 *Knight of Thistle* emerged from the North British Locomotive Co. in July 1924. It is photographed in a filthy state at the engine hoist, which was located at the west side of the new engine shed at Grantham. No. 60065, as LNER 2564 *Knight of the Thistle*, was at Doncaster Works for a general repair when the nameplates were replaced. The new ones state the name as *Knight of Thistle* and are seen here. It remains unknown why 'the' was dropped from the nameplate. The locomotive was rebuilt to A3 Class in March 1947 and is seen here with a double chimney, which was fitted in October 1958. The locomotive was withdrawn from New England in June 1964.

Grantham 60021

Gresley Class A4 4-6-2 locomotive no. 60021 *Wild Swan* is at Grantham Station. Designed for high speed services between London and Newcastle, thirty-five of the locomotives in the class were built at Doncaster between 1935 and 1938. *Wild Swan,* entering traffic in February 1938, is operating 'The Elizabethan' non-stop express passenger service between Edinburgh Waverley and London King's Cross, which started in the early 1950s and ceased in the early 1960s. No. 60021 worked the service from King's Cross shed, where it was allocated from June 1950 until June 1963, when it moved to New England. It was withdrawn four months later in October.

Grantham 61389

The North British Locomotive Co., Queens Park Works, built Thompson Class 4-6-0 locomotive no. 61389 in November 1951. The B1s were intended to replace the numerous types of classes that had few parts in common and that were operated by the LNER at the time. Thus, the locomotives incorporated a large number of standardised components to reduce costs and they were used for both passenger and goods services. In total 410 of the locomotives were manufactured between 1942 and 1952. No. 61389 is passing through Grantham Station on a goods service. The locomotive was allocated to Grantham for six years between October 1957 and September 1963 and would have worked local branch passenger services. It was withdrawn from Frodingham in May 1965.

Grantham 60050

Gresley Class A1 Pacific locomotive no. 60050 *Persimmon* was built at Doncaster Works in October 1924 and entered service as LNER no. 2549. The A1s were designed for express passenger services on the East Coast Main Line and fifty-two were built between 1922 and 1924. Twenty-seven more were erected between 1928 and 1935, with a predominantly similar design, slightly modified and classified A3. No. 60050 was rebuilt to A3 specifications in December 1943 and received a double chimney in April 1959. Converted to left-hand drive in September 1952, *Persimmon* had five spells at Grantham, the longest being for almost fifteen years between July 1927 and January 1942. The last was six years from September 1956 to June 1962. It was withdrawn from New England in June 1963.

Grantham 69552

At the engine hoist at Grantham new engine shed is Class N2 0-6-2T locomotive no. 69552. The hoist was installed next to the new engine shed when it was built in 1897, replacing a set of shear-legs that were located adjacent to the old engine shed on the site of the old turntable. They were installed in that position when the turntable was moved in 1889. No. 69552 was designed by Gresley and entered service from Beyer, Peacock & Co. in March 1925. Sixty locomotives of the design had been built before Grouping for the GNR. Forty-seven were built afterwards, including no. 69552 (as LNER no. 2585), and the last one was erected in 1929. Built with the intention of working on the London suburban services, they also found themselves on similar duties in cities around the country. No. 69552 was at Grantham from November 1958 to May 1960, at which time it was condemned.

Grantham D208

British Rail Class 40 diesel locomotive D208 was built at Vulcan Foundry by the English Electric Co. in August 1958. It was part of the initial order for ten and subsequently 190 more locomotives were built, with the last completed in 1962. They were built to replace pacific locomotives on the main routes, and despite problems on the East Coast Main Line, found favour on the west coast line. D208 is depicted in the original livery; in time the front end would be painted yellow and from 1966 the livery was changed to blue. At the TOPS renumbering the locomotive received no. 40 008 in February 1974. The locomotive was removed from service in November 1982 and subsequently scrapped at Crewe Works.

Grantham 60517

Grantham Station was opened between July and August 1852, accommodating the Great Northern Railway and the Ambergate, Nottingham, Boston & Eastern Junction Railway. It replaced a temporary terminus at Old Wharf, opened by the latter company in July 1850. Thompson A2/3 Pacific locomotive no. 60517 *Ocean Swell* was erected at Doncaster during November 1946, entering service at Heaton where it spent much of its career. From there the locomotive was employed on main line goods and passenger services between the capital cities and also to Leeds. *Ocean Swell* was sent to Tweedmouth in October 1961 to work goods trains and to act as standby for failures. It was withdrawn from there in November 1962.

Grantham 60134

Leaving Grantham Station's Platform 1 is Peppercorn Class A1 4-6-2 locomotive no. 60134 *Foxhunter*. Designs for the class commenced while Edward Thompson was Chief Mechanical Engineer in 1944, however, when he retired in 1946, a final design had yet to be completed. The reigns were taken up by A. H. Peppercorn who kept some of Thompson's mechanical arrangements but returned to a conventional front bogie. Forty-eight of the engines were built between 1948 and 1949 at Doncaster and Darlington Works. No. 60134 *Foxhunter* was built at Darlington in November 1948 and allocated to Copley Hill. The shed was initially allocated five A1s but after reorganisation in the early 1950s, this was increased to ten. No. 60134 worked from the Leeds area all its life, having spells at Ardsley and Neville Hill in the early 1960s before being withdrawn in October 1965.

Grantham 60024

Gresley Class A4 Pacific locomotive no. 60024 *Falcon* is leaving Platform 1 at Grantham Station. The engine looks resplendent in the British Railway's livery of green with black and orange lining, which was applied for the first time in December 1952 and continued until withdrawal in October 1963. Yet, *Falcon* had a number of livery changes during its time in service. It began in February 1937 as LNER no. 4484, with a livery of green with black and white lining. However, the black at the front did not join the curve in the position seen here; it went further back and stopped just to the left of the nameplate at the first boiler casing joint. This was changed to the traditional pattern by early 1938.

Grantham 60017

The last of the first four Gresley A4s ordered (and to carry 'silver' in its name) was no. 60017 *Silver Fox,* built at Doncaster Works in December 1935. The first four A4s were built specifically to run the 'Silver Jubilee' service, which operated between London and Newcastle. To fit with the service name, 'silver' was incorporated in the locomotives' names. Also, their livery initially reflected the silver theme, with three shades of grey being used along with the black front, until it was changed to blue in November 1937. On the side of the locomotive there is a stainless steel fox. This was carried by the locomotive from new and was made by Samuel Fox & Co. of Sheffield. The locomotive was the last of the 'silver' named A4s to be withdrawn in October 1963.

Grantham 60136

Peppercorn Class A1 4-6-2 locomotive no. 60136 *Alcazar* was photographed on the main line near Grantham Station. Built at Darlington Works in November 1948, the locomotive entered service at Copley Hill. It was fitted with a diagram 118 boiler when new and carried four different boilers of this type throughout its career. In March 1961 it received a diagram 117 boiler from Thompson A2/3 no. 60514 *Chamossaire* and the original boiler for no. 60521 *Watling Street*. The two boilers were very similar with the dome and weight being different. The diagram 117 boiler usually had a round dome, whereas the 118 diagram boiler had a banjo dome. However, a dummy banjo dome could be fitted to the round dome boiler so telling them apart was difficult, but possible by the position of the dummy banjo dome placed further forward than normal. In this instance the diagram 118 boiler is fitted. The locomotive was withdrawn in May 1963 and scrapped at Doncaster.

Grantham 60139

Peppercorn Class A1 4-6-2 locomotive no. 60139 *Sea Eagle*, built at Darlington in December 1948, was withdrawn from Doncaster in June 1964. The engine ran for eighteen months until May 1950 without being named. Upon introduction of the Peppercorn Class A1s, only the first locomotive was to be named, which was no. 60114 *W. P. Allen*. However, this decision was reversed and all had been named by mid-1952. The *Sea Eagle* name had previously been carried by Class A4 locomotive LNER no. 4487 (later BR 60028) until October 1947 when it became *Walter K. Whigham*.

Grantham 69814

Class A5 4-6-2T locomotive no. 69814, built at Gorton Works in December 1912, was formerly no. 129 and part of the Great Central Railway's 9N Class, designed by J. Robinson. Forty-four locomotives were built at both Gorton Works and Hawthorn, Leslie & Co. over a period of fifteen years beginning in 1911. The locomotives erected in 1912 had the size of their superheaters increased by six elements to 24. This was subsequently altered to 22 before Grouping. The locomotive is seen on the main line near Grantham and has been fitted with windows on the side of the cab; originally the cab was open. This modification was implemented in March 1924. The locomotive was one of the last three of the class to be removed from service in November 1960.

Grantham 60118

Peppercorn Class A1 4-6-2 locomotive no. 60118 *Archibald Sturrock* was photographed at the south east end of Grantham shed and in front of the old coal stage and mechanical coal stage. The water softener is on the right. The old coal stage was added when the new shed was built in 1897, and was replaced by the mechanical coal stage in 1937. The latter had a 200-ton capacity and was built and installed by Henry Lees & Co. costing close to £6,000. The water softener was the first structure to be demolished when the site was cleared in 1964, followed by the mechanical coal stage and finally by the old coal stage in 1965. No. 60118 was built at Doncaster in November 1948 and allocated to Copley Hill. It was withdrawn from Neville Hill in October 1965.

Grantham 60153

Peppercorn Class A1 4-6-2 locomotive no. 60153 *Flamboyant* entered service from Doncaster Works in August 1949. It is photographed in between coal stacks located to the east of the new engine shed at Grantham. A York engine throughout its time in service, *Flamboyant* was one of five A1s equipped with Timken roller bearings on all axles. It was also one of three A1s to be withdrawn in November 1962.

Grantham 60048

Gresley Class A1 Pacific, later A3 (May 1946), no. 60048 *Doncaster* was built at Doncaster Works in August 1924. The locomotive is seen at Platform 1 at Grantham Station in an absolutely filthy condition, looking like it is still painted in the wartime black livery rather than BR green! When this photograph was taken, *Doncaster* was a Grantham engine with two spells there at the beginning of its career and two at the end. It had three spells at Doncaster, one of fourteen years from October 1935 to February 1949 and one seven years from November 1953 to June 1958. It was withdrawn in September 1963 and scrapped at Doncaster by the end of the month.

Grantham 69827

Class A5 4-6-2T locomotive no. 69827 entered traffic from Gorton Works (as GCR Class 9N) in May 1923. Ten locomotives in the class were built in 1923 and were ordered by the GCR before Grouping. They were originally built for use on London suburban services that operated out of Marylebone Station, which is why the engines were based at Neasden. No. 69827 (as LNER no. 5154) was a long-term resident at the shed, staying thirty-one years before being transferred to Grantham in May 1954. From Grantham the locomotive would have worked passenger services to Derby and Nottingham. It was withdrawn in November 1959.

Grantham 68626

Seen next to the stack of coal at the south-east end of Grantham shed is Class J69 0-6-0T locomotive no. 68626. It was built at Stratford Works in June 1904 for the GER, being classified as S56. Twenty were built for passenger work, all in 1904, and were based on GER Class R24, but featured increased boiler pressure and improved water tank capacity. The locomotive was at Grantham for two years between May 1958 and May 1960, moving to Colwick and Stratford before withdrawal in May 1962.

Grantham 60066

A smart looking Gresley Class A1 4-6-2 locomotive, no. 60066 *Merry Hampton,* is at Grantham's Platform 1. It was built by the North British Locomotive Co. in August 1924 and entered service as LNER no. 2565. In May 1926 the locomotive was involved in a derailment at Cramlington, 9 miles from Newcastle, which thankfully did not result in any serious injuries. The locomotive was back in traffic towards the end of the year. It was rebuilt to A3 specifications in December 1945. Before it became Class A3 it was predominantly allocated to Scottish region sheds, but after moving from Edinburgh Haymarket in August 1950, it spent the rest of its career in England. Doncaster and King's Cross were its more frequent homes, with stays at New England and Grantham in the late 1950s and early 1960s. It was withdrawn in September 1963.

Grantham 'Deltic'

British Railways DP1 (Diesel Prototype no. 1) *Deltic* is pausing at Grantham Station. The locomotive was built by English Electric Co. in 1955 as a prototype for British Railways and was tested both on the west coast and east coast main lines. The locomotive was fitted with two Deltic engines, each producing 1,650 hp. British Railways ordered twenty-two locomotives to the design and these were produced between 1961 and 1962, becoming British Railways Class 55 locomotives. They went on to have a twenty-year career operating East Coast Main Line services, until they were replaced by high speed trains in the 1980s. *Deltic* was removed from service in March 1961 and was donated to the London Science Museum. It is currently housed at Locomotion, Shildon.

Lincoln 61272

The Midland Railway was the first railway company to operate from Lincoln, opening St Marks
Station in 1846. The Manchester, Sheffield & Lincolnshire began to operate services from the
station in 1848. The GNR service to Lincoln started in October 1848 operating from Lincoln
Central Station. At the station the first shed was erected but only lasted six months. A second
shed was opened in 1851 and extended in 1857 to accommodate four engines. The North British
Locomotive Co. built Thompson Class B1 4-6-0 locomotive no. 61272 in December 1947. It is seen
here at Lincoln GNR shed yard with the crew accommodation block, erected around 1954, just
behind the tender. No. 61272 was withdrawn in January 1965 and became a stationary boiler for
the heating of passenger carriages. It was transferred to departmental stock and received no. 25. It
was finally condemned in November 1965 and scrapped.

Lincoln 69808

In the early 1870s the GNR bought land on the Holme from Lincoln Corporation to build a new
engine shed. At the time the GNR was causing disruption to the town because the movements of
the engines around the station necessitated the closing of level crossings on main roads. A new
four-road shed with space for twelve engines was built in 1875 to solve the problems. Robinson
Class A5 4-6-2T locomotive no. 69808 seen here in the shed yard, was built at Gorton Works in
August 1911; the last of the first batch of ten to be built. As GCR no. 448, the locomotive was one
of eight in the first ten originally fitted with a Schmidt superheater, whereas the other two were fitted
with one of Robinson's own design. The Schmidt superheaters fitted between 1915 and 1917 were
replaced with the Robinson type. The locomotive was withdrawn in November 1960. Lincoln shed
closed to steam in October 1964.

Lincoln Pyewipe Junction Sidings 61742

Gresley Class K2 2-6-0 locomotive no. 61742, built at Doncaster Works in May 1916 was photographed at Lincoln Pyewipe Junction sidings. When it was built, the engine formed part of GNR Class H3, and sixty-five of the locomotives were constructed between 1914 and 1921. The locomotive design was based on GCR Class H2 with modifications. These included a larger boiler, Robinson 24-element superheater (increased from the 18-element Schmidt superheater previously used) and larger pony truck wheels. The locomotive was at a variety of sheds throughout its career until its withdrawal from New England shed in May 1962.

Lincoln Pyewipe Junction Sidings 68528

Lincoln Pyewipe Junction was located to the west of Lincoln. It was also where the GNR and GER joint line to Doncaster met the old Lancashire, Derbyshire & East Coast Railway line, which became part of the GCR to Chesterfield and Sheffield. Two sheds were located close to the junction, one built by the LD&ECR in 1897 and one for the GER; this was opened in 1886. Seen at the sidings is J67/1 no. 68528, built at Stratford in March 1892. It was rebuilt to J69/1 in December 1903, keeping these modifications until it was withdrawn from Lincoln in October 1959.

Lincoln Pyewipe Junction Sidings 64961

Gresley Class J39 0-6-0 locomotive no. 64961 was erected at Darlington Works in June 1938. The locomotive is equipped with the group standard tender, which had a capacity of 4,200 gallons and over 7 tons of coal. It has riveted straight sides and is displaying the early BR emblem. The class received black livery throughout its time in service. No. 64961 was withdrawn from Lincoln in October 1959 after a nine-month allocation. The locomotive had previously been at Retford (twelve years) and had numerous spells at Ardsley (allocated when new) and Doncaster.

Retford 68530

Retford's first Great Northern shed was situated at Retford Station close to Platform 2 (the down platform) and opened in 1851 with two roads. As traffic increased, a new shed with improved facilities was required. It was opened in March 1875 and sited west of the station. The shed consisted of four dead-end roads; the construction costing around £5,400. At the west side of Retford's Great Northern shed is Class J69/1 0-6-0 locomotive no. 68530, built at Stratford Works in March 1892 as GER Class R24. The locomotive was rebuilt in January 1905 and withdrawn from Retford shed in February 1961.

Retford 63926

The first railway to run into Retford was the Manchester, Sheffield & Lincolnshire Railway, which opened a line between Woodhouse Junction, Sheffield, and Gainsborough in July 1849. The Great Northern Railway Company's first service appeared in September 1849 with the main line connection following in August 1852. Gresley Class O2 2-8-0 locomotive no. 63926, seen here at Retford shed, was built at the North British Locomotive Co., Atlas Works, during May 1921, and was allocated to New England. Retford was the locomotive's last shed, arriving in February 1952 and staying eleven years. It was removed from service in September 1963 and sold for scrap to Bulwell Forest Wagon Works.

Retford 60055

Retford Station is approximately 138½ miles from London King's Cross. On the southern approach to the station the line falls at a gradient of 1 in 178 before becoming level. Just past the station the line rises at 1 in 440 for a short distance before falling at 1 in 198 and then becoming level. Gresley Class A1 4-6-2 locomotive no. 60055 *Woolwinder* is pictured on the main line just outside Retford. Built at Doncaster Works during December 1924, the locomotive was rebuilt to A3 Class between April and June 1942. It is pictured with the double chimney that it received in June 1958. The locomotive was one of twenty-two of the class not to receive smoke deflectors. Withdrawn from King's Cross shed in September 1961, the engine was later scrapped at Doncaster.

Doncaster 63934

Gresley Class o2 2-8-0 locomotive no. 63934 was built at Doncaster in November 1923 – after Grouping – with a slight modification to the cab so that it conformed to the Composite Load Gauge. The shape of the roof was altered, as was the position of the whistle, which moved from the cab roof; a shorter chimney was also fitted. These alterations brought the locomotive into part two of the o2 class. Entering service at New England, no. 63934 was employed on coal trains destined for the London area. There was a long spell at Doncaster between June 1954 and October 1960, after which the engine was transferred to Retford. Withdrawal from the latter came in July 1962.

Doncaster 90732

Photographed in front of the old north coal stage at Doncaster shed is War Department 'Austerity' 2-8-0 locomotive no. 90732 *Vulcan*. The locomotive was built at Vulcan Foundry, Newton-le-Willows, in May 1945 for the War Department, for use in Europe. The North British Locomotive Co. built 545 engines, with Vulcan Foundry adding 390. As WD no. 79312, the locomotive was the last to be built at the Vulcan Foundry Works and had the distinction of being the only member of the class to be named. The engine was at Doncaster from March 1957 until January 1960, moving to Frodingham, where it saw out the remainder of its career. Withdrawal came in September 1962 after being in store for five months.

Doncaster D5525

British Railways Class 30 diesel-electric locomotive no. D5525 (no. 31107 from January 1973) was built in April 1959 at Brush Traction, Loughborough. The engine is seen at Doncaster Plant Works with Class 26 no. D5320 to the left and Class 21 no. D6109 on the right. D5525 was part of a second order for forty locomotives after the initial twenty proved successful. Further orders were placed and by the early 1960s the class total had reached 263. The engine was rebuilt in September 1965 to Class 31, surviving until withdrawal in October 2008 when it was scrapped. D6109 was withdrawn after a collision in 1968, while D5320 was in service until October 1991.

Doncaster 61950

Doncaster Plant Works was built in 1853 by the GNR for repairs and maintenance to locomotives and rolling stock. Construction of locomotives did not begin until 1866 when the GNR changed its policy of acquiring locomotives from contractors. Gresley Class K3 2-6-0 locomotive no. 61950 is seen here at Doncaster Works in April 1959. The engine was built in September 1935 by the North British Locomotive Co. and had slightly modified features from earlier engines. These included vacuum brakes, stool seats, modified sanding apparatus and larger diameter steam pipes. The standard LNER livery for the class was black with red lining; BR added white to this combination. Removal from service came in November 1962 when the engine was allocated at Doncaster.

Doncaster Departmental Number 4

Sentinel Class Y1 0-4-0T shunting locomotive was photographed adjacent to the Doncaster Works Crimpsall repair shop. The locomotive differed from later Y1 Class engines as it had a smaller boiler and slight variations in detail. It entered service in October 1926 and remained unnumbered until the early part of 1930, acquiring no. 4801, which was later changed to 4991 (September 1937). The locomotive was first allocated to Boston Hall Hills Sleeper Depot, where it spent almost fourteen years. In February 1940 it moved to Retford, but stayed only two months, going into store at Doncaster Works. In February 1948 its final home became Ranskill Wagon Works, where it received the BR number 68132 in May 1948 and became Departmental No. 4 in December 1952. It was withdrawn in June 1959.

Doncaster 69452

On the scrap line in April 1959 is Ivatt N1 Class 0-6-2T locomotive no. 69452. Built for the GNR in December 1910, the engine was one of fifty-six produced to the design. The intention was for them to work on the London suburban passenger services but they could also be found on freight duties around the capital. As LNER no. 4752, the locomotive was part of a group of nine class members fitted with superheaters by the company in the mid-1920s. It received the apparatus in February 1925. In GNR days two locomotives had been fitted with Schmidt superheaters, but were later brought in line with the others and received those to Robinson's design. No. 69452 was among the remains of the class withdrawn in March 1959, with the last two going in April.

Doncaster 70013

British Railways Standard Class 7 4-6-2 locomotive no. 70013 *Oliver Cromwell* is pictured at Doncaster in May 1959. The engine was built at Crewe Works in May 1951 and allocated to Norwich where it spent the best part of the 1950s having only a transfer to Ipswich and back. It moved to March shed in September 1961 and started a tour of the Carlisle sheds in late 1963. *Oliver Cromwell* was allocated to Norwich at the time of this visit to Doncaster Works, which received the responsibility for major repairs on Eastern Region Class 7 engines in 1956. It had previously been solely the duty of Crewe Works. *Oliver Cromwell* was the last of the class to be withdrawn in August 1968. It went into the national collection and was housed at Bressingham. It has since been restored to full working condition.

Doncaster 61655

Built at Darlington in April 1936 Gresley Class B17 4-6-0 locomotive no. 61655 *Middlesbrough* fell into part four of the class as it had a 4,200-gallon tender with straight sides. The engine was fitted with a diagram 100A boiler in July 1950, entering part six of the class. Stratford, Gorton and Darlington had all been responsible for the maintenance of the class before Doncaster took up the task in 1951. The locomotive was withdrawn in April 1959 and is seen here at Doncaster Works in May, waiting to be scrapped.

Doncaster 64176

GNR Class J22, LNER Class J6 0-6-0 locomotive no. 64176 is seen at Doncaster Works. The engine was built in the first batch of fifteen that emerged from Doncaster between August and December 1911 and entered service as GNR no. 527 in November 1911. The locomotive was built with a Schmidt-type superheater, but by 1930 the standard for the class had become the Robinson-type, with both types having eighteen elements. No. 64176 was also built with Ramsbottom safety valves, however, they were also replaced in the 1920s by Ross pop safety valves. During BR days the engine was allocated to Peterborough New England shed and was withdrawn from there in March 1959. Scrapping took place at Doncaster and could be what the locomotive was awaiting when the picture was taken.

Doncaster 60800

Gresley Class V2 2-6-2 locomotive no. 60800 *Green Arrow* is pictured at Doncaster, where it was the first of the class to be constructed in June 1936. It was one of eight locomotives named, taking its own name from the registered goods service that had just been introduced. Of the others, five engines received names of army regiments and two of schools. *Green Arrow* was allocated to King's Cross shed for the majority of its career, only spending a month at Woodford between May and June 1953. It was withdrawn in August 1962 and preserved; it currently resides at the NRM.

Doncaster 60700

Gresley's W1 Class 4-6-4 locomotive was originally built with a water-tube boiler but only existed in this form for eight years before being rebuilt. This occurred at Doncaster between October 1936 and November 1937, retaining the frames but receiving similar parts fitted to other Gresley engines. The cylinders were based on the A1s, the boiler on the P2/3 diagram 108 and it was streamlined like the A4 Class. The engine was allocated mainly to two sheds, King's Cross and Doncaster, with a month at Haymarket in mid-1942. Despite showing promising performances on the services allocated, it was never free from the niggling problems that had beset it since conception. It is seen here at Doncaster in August 1958 as BR no. 60700. It was withdrawn in June 1959 and scrapped at Doncaster.

Doncaster 60506

Originally built at Doncaster Works in September 1936 as a member of Gresley's P2 Class, *Wolf of Badenoch* was rebuilt at the town's works in May 1944 to Thompson's Class A2/2, becoming a 4-6-2 locomotive and numbered 60506. Rebuilding was initiated as a result of various components failing when the P2s were operating the Edinburgh to Aberdeen route. The locomotives were originally built to run in Scotland so their names were chosen to reflect this. 'Wolf of Badenoch' was the nickname for the Earl of Buchan, who in the 1300s caused much disorder in the north-east of Scotland. The locomotive was withdrawn from New England in April 1961 and scrapped at Doncaster.

Doncaster 60514

When Doncaster Carr loco shed was opened in 1876, two coal stages were provided at either end of the shed yard. The north stage was rebuilt in 1898 to provide a space for the drivers and to improve productivity. When the mechanical coaler was installed in around 1926, the north stage was retained while the southern one was demolished. Thompson Class A2/3 4-6-2 locomotive no. 60514 *Chamossaire* is seen near the old north coal stage at the shed in September 1958. The engine was built at Doncaster in September 1946 and allocated to King's Cross. No. 60514's only other allocation was to New England in December 1948. *Chamossaire* was at Doncaster Works for a Heavy/Intermediate repair from the end of July to the end of August 1958, but returned for eleven days at the end of September for a non-classified repair. It saw four more years' service before withdrawal in December 1962, but was not scrapped until mid-1963.

Doncaster 60004

An interesting sight at Doncaster shed is Gresley Class A4 4-6-2 locomotive no. 60004 *William Whitelaw*, minus middle driving wheel. The engine was built at Doncaster in December 1937 and allocated to King's Cross, closely followed by a move to Gateshead. When entering service as LNER no. 4462 it was originally named *Great Snipe*. The change to *William Whitelaw* came in June 1941; the name was taken from A1 no. 2563 (later BR no. 60064), which became *Tagalie*. *William Whitelaw* was a Haymarket engine at the time of this photograph. It was allocated there from July 1941 to June 1963, apart from a three-month spell at Aberdeen in June 1962. The engine saw further service at Aberdeen after leaving Haymarket, but was finally withdrawn in July 1966.

Doncaster 60889

The original engine shed was located at Doncaster Station and had space for thirty locomotives. The allocation to Doncaster far exceeded this capacity and by the mid to late 1860s more space was sought; it was found about a mile south of Doncaster Station, but the land was of poor quality and required a large amount of attention before it could be utilised. Work started in May 1874 but it was not until March 1876 that the shed was finally opened. The cost of the works totalled £37,000. This Gresley Class V2 2-6-2 locomotive no. 60889, pictured at the north end of Doncaster Carr shed during 1959, was built at Darlington in December 1939. It was allocated to Doncaster at the time of the picture and had been resident since April 1947. It was withdrawn from Doncaster in June 1963.

Doncaster 60144

When built, Doncaster shed was 420 ft by 180 ft and equipped with twelve roads open at each end with space for up to 100 locomotives. Water for use at Doncaster shed was initially obtained from the River Don, however, by the early 1900s this had become so polluted it was no longer fit for use in the engines. Supplies were then acquired from the River Idle, 8 miles away, which was pumped to the shed, the connection costing close to £20,000. Peppercorn Class A1 Pacific no. 60144 *King's Courier* is seen at Doncaster Carr engine shed taking on water. The engine was allocated to Doncaster when new in March 1949, moving to various sheds before returning in November 1957. Withdrawal from Doncaster shed came in April 1963.

Doncaster 60857

At the south end of Doncaster Carr engine shed is Gresley V2 Class 2-6-2 locomotive no. 60857. It was built at Darlington Works in May 1939 and numbered 4828, with its first allocation being to Gorton shed. The locomotive's first spell at Doncaster lasted two months between January and March 1940, when it moved to Sheffield for a six-year stay. The engine then returned to Doncaster in September 1946 and was allocated to the shed for the rest of its career, apart from a four-month allocation to Grantham between June and October 1960. No. 60857 is missing some of its motion and the right-hand piston and could be under repair, being close to the shed fitting shop, which is seen behind the locomotive. It left service in April 1962 and went straight for scrap, which took place at Doncaster Works.

Doncaster 63973

Replenishing its water reserves at the south end of Doncaster Carr shed is Gresley Class O2 2-8-0 locomotive no. 63973. The engine was built at Doncaster Works in October 1942 as the first in a batch of ten completed between October and December of that year. No. 63973 (as LNER no. 3843) was built to group standard specifications, but with a side window fitted in the cab. When new the locomotive was attached to a group standard 4,200 gallon tender with space for over 7 tons of coal. The tender has stepped-out sides and was requisitioned from a Class D49 due to material shortages during the War. Twenty-three were so equipped with a variation being some tenders had straight sides. The locomotive left service from Retford in September 1963.

Doncaster D6102

Pictured at Doncaster Works is Class 21 diesel-electric locomotive no. D6102, built by the North British Locomotive Co. in December 1958 as part of an order of ten for the Pilot Scheme. The engine was intended to work on the London suburban passenger services and eventually fifty-eight were constructed for work in the south. However, problems with the engines plagued their time in service and the whole class were allocated to Scotland in 1960 for the NBLC to fix the problems. Twenty, including D6102 in May 1966, received a new type of engine, becoming Class 29, but these also experienced significant problems. The original locomotives had all been withdrawn by 1968 and the Class 29s, with D6102, were gone by October 1971.

Doncaster 69450

An Ivatt N1 is waiting to be scrapped at Doncaster Works. The locomotive was built at Doncaster in May 1910 for the GNR, the final one from a batch of ten built between March and May. All but four of the class were fitted with condensing equipment when new. This was subsequently removed from some of the engines as they were transferred from London to Yorkshire. No. 69450 was one of the last engines to have the apparatus removed in January 1953 while at Copley Hill. This latter shed saw the locomotive's withdrawal in March 1959.

Doncaster 60122

Doncaster shed was originally allocated five Peppercorn A1s. However, by 1950 all had been transferred to either King's Cross, Grantham or Copley Hill as they were not needed on Doncaster based services. Thirteen of the class were eventually allocated to Doncaster during the late 1950s as diesel locomotives took over the mainline passenger services. Peppercorn Class A1 Pacific locomotive no. 60122 *Curlew* entered traffic from Doncaster Works in December 1948. The engine was allocated to Doncaster shed in April 1959 and withdrawn from there in December 1962.

Doncaster 61812

Gresley 2-6-0 locomotive no. 61812 was erected at Darlington in August 1924 as a K3/2. These differed from the earlier locomotives as they had an altered chimney, dome and whistle, and a cab with side windows attached to a group standard tender. The locomotive is seen here with a GN tender with coal rails, which it acquired around March 1927. This was due to it being allocated to Scotland where the original group standard tender would have been too long for the turntables found there. A total of ten engines had GN tenders during their time in service, with some reverting to the group standard one; however, most retained it until withdrawn. No. 61812 was still attached to one when withdrawn in September 1962 from Doncaster.

Doncaster 67787

At Doncaster shed is Thompson Class L1 2-6-4T locomotive no. 67787, erected at Robert Stephenson & Hawthorns in April 1950. A hundred locomotives were built at various works; one for the LNER, the rest entering service for BR. No. 67787 was the first L1 allocated to the Norwich area. It was based at Ipswich shed from August 1950 working passenger services in the area, and moved to Neasden in March 1953. In May 1959, when this picture was taken, the engine was allocated to King's Cross and it had been there since September 1958. In October 1960 it became a Doncaster engine before final allocation to Colwick. It left service from there in December 1962.

Doncaster 60123

Doncaster Works erected Peppercorn Class A1 4-6-2 locomotive no. 60123 *H. A. Ivatt* in February 1949. When new the locomotive was fitted with a diagram 118 boiler, it had three cylinders measuring 19 inches by 26 inches, and Walschaerts valve gear with piston valves measuring 10 inches. The locomotive was named after the GNR superintendant in a ceremony at Doncaster in July 1950, which was performed by his son H.G. Ivatt. The locomotive has the distinction of being the first of the class to be withdrawn in October 1962, which occurred after derailment at Offord in September while on a goods service. It was scrapped at Doncaster.

Doncaster 60114

Doncaster Works built the first Peppercorn Class A1 4-6-2 locomotive – no. 60114 *W. P. Allen* – in August 1948. The engine was named in October at a ceremony at King's Cross. The first sixteen locomotives were fitted with Flaman speed indicators, the bracket for which is located at the rear of the running plate. These were removed in the early 1950s; however, the bracket often remained in situ. Smith-Stone speed indicators were fitted to all except one of the class in the early 1960s and these were attached to the other side of the locomotive. No. 60114 was withdrawn from Copley Hill in November 1962 and scrapped at Doncaster by mid-1963.

Doncaster 60090

Outside the Weigh House at Doncaster Works in August 1959 is Gresley A3 Pacific no. 60090 *Grand Parade* looking fresh from the paint shop. The new Weigh House was built in 1935 between the Crimpsall repair shop and the paint shop after the old Weigh House near Doncaster station had become outdated. LNER no. 2744 entered service to King's Cross in August 1928, but the original locomotive was damaged beyond repair in the Castlecary accident on 10 December 1937. A new locomotive entered service as no. 2744 in April 1938. At the time of the picture, no. 60090 was in works for heavy intermediate repairs. It arrived at the beginning of July and did not leave until mid-September. *Grand Parade* had a further four years in service before its withdrawal in October 1963 to be cut-up at Cowlairs. This was completed by January 1964.

CHAPTER 3
Barnsley to York

Barnsley 69268

Class N5 0-6-2T locomotive no. 69268 is seen at Barnsley GCR shed. The engine was built by Beyer, Peacock & Co. in January 1894. One hundred and twenty-nine were built between 1891 and 1901 for the Manchester, Sheffield & Lincolnshire Railway, which later became the GCR, forming Classes 9C, 9F and 9O. No. 69268 was built as part of the 9F class and these engines had modified valve gear from the earlier 9C engines, which were erected as prototypes. Barnsley had a large contingent of N5s during LNER and BR days and these operated local passenger services. No. 69268 was withdrawn in January 1960.

Barnsley 67445

Barnsley GCR shed was built by the Lancashire & Yorkshire Railway at the east side of Barnsley Station and it consisted of two tracks open at each end. It closed at the start of 1964 and was subsequently demolished. GCR Class 9L 4-4-2T locomotive no. 1125, built at Beyer, Peacock & Co. in May 1907, was one of only twelve produced. At Grouping the engine became LNER Class C14 and it acquired the number 6125 in May 1925. Allocation at Barnsley came in July 1957 to work local passenger services; it was the locomotive's swansong before its withdrawal at the end of 1959.

Wakefield 61115

At Wakefield shed in April 1967 is Thompson Class B1 4-6-0 locomotive no. 61115. The shed was located to the south of Wakefield Kirkgate Station and built by the Lancashire & Yorkshire Railway in 1893. It was constructed in brick and had ten roads, which were dead ends but were later altered to through roads. No. 61115 entered traffic from the North British Locomotive Co. in January 1947 and was allocated to York. The engine arrived at Wakefield in November 1966 and was a month away from being condemned for scrap at the time of this photograph. Wakefield shed closed in June 1967 and subsequently was used as a wagon shop. Demolition came in 1993, followed in 1994 by Wakefield power station, seen in the background of this picture.

Hull 67682

Pictured near Hull Paragon Station is Gresley Class V3 2-6-2T locomotive no. 67682, built in September 1939. The V3s were similar to the V1 Class but with boiler pressure increased to 200 psi. No. 67682 was one of only ten built as a V3, but V1s were converted to V3 between 1952 and 1961, eventually totalling fifty-nine. The locomotive was initially allocated to Gateshead where it would have worked the Newcastle to Middlesbrough service, but it could also find itself on journeys to Carlisle. No. 67682 was sent to Hull from Blaydon in January 1959, staying in the area until returning north-east to Darlington in November 1961. September 1963 saw the engine leave service.

Hull 60080

At Hull Paragon Station is Gresley Class A1 4-6-2 locomotive no. 60080 *Dick Turpin*. The engine was erected at North British Locomotive Co. in November 1924 and rebuilt to A3 in November 1942. It is seen with a double chimney acquired in October 1959 and two years later it received smoke deflectors. It was an uncommon occurrence for a Pacific to be at Hull because of the sharp curves at the station. However, towards the end of their working life it was possible for them to end up anywhere on a variety of services. Leeds-based engines sometimes worked to Hull, and as *Dick Turpin* was at a Leeds shed between 1960 and 1963, at Holbeck, Ardsley and Neville Hill, it could explain this appearance. It was withdrawn from Gateshead in October 1964.

Selby 63348

Class Q6 0-8-0 locomotive no. 63348 was built at Darlington Works in March 1913. It was originally a member of NER Class T2 designed by Vincent Raven and was built to operate mineral services. One hundred and twenty examples of the design were produced between 1913 and 1921. From 1938 the class started to receive diagram 50A boilers together with the original diagram 50 boilers. No. 63348 was fitted with a diagram 50A in September 1946 and carried one until withdrawal from Neville Hill in June 1964. The locomotive had two spells at Selby in BR days. The first allocation was between December 1949 and February 1953 and the second stretched from July 1957 to September 1959.

Selby 61459

Selby's first shed was opened by the Leeds & Selby Railway in 1834. In 1871 this was displaced by another built south of the station by the NER. It was a square roundhouse and in 1898 a new facility of the same type was opened next to the existing one. Class B16 4-6-0 locomotive no. 61459, built at Darlington in November 1923, was ordered by the NER to be part of their Class S3, designed by Raven. Some of the engines were rebuilt by Gresley and Thompson but no. 61459 remained in its original form. It was resident at Selby from July 1957 until June 1959, a few months before the shed closed to steam in September 1959. No. 61459 was withdrawn from York in September 1961.

Selby 43071
LMS Class 4 2-6-0 locomotive no. 43071 emerged from Darlington Works in August 1950. Three works were involved in the construction of the class; Horwich (75), Doncaster (50) and Darlington (37). The locomotive's initial allocation was to Darlington shed spending its first five years there before moving around various sheds in the North East. It arrived at Selby from Thornaby in November 1958 and was allocated there for less than a year before a stint at York. A further three moves were undertaken before the locomotive was withdrawn in March 1967.

Selby 63429
Looking the worse for wear at Selby shed is Class Q6 0-8-0 locomotive no. 63429, built by Armstrong, Whitworth in May 1920. When new, the locomotive was attached to a 4,125-gallon self-trimming tender with curved coal rails. However, as the result of a complicated exchange of tenders between classes, the locomotive was given a tender from a C7 Class locomotive. No. 63429 (as LNER no. 2272) received it, after slight modifications, from C7 Class no. 710 during February 1932. The locomotive was withdrawn from Tyne Dock in July 1967.

Leeds 60084
Gresley Class A3 4-6-2 locomotive no. 60084 *Trigo* is at Neville Hill shed, Leeds. Built at Doncaster in February 1930, the engine entered service as LNER no. 2595 at Gateshead. It is seen here after being fitted with a double chimney and smoke deflectors, which were attached in October 1959 and November 1961 respectively. *Trigo* is coupled with a streamlined non-corridor tender (no. 5645), after originally being paired with a new-type non-corridor tender (no. 5476). The original recipient of tender no. 5645 was LNER no. 2558 *Tracery* in June 1937. Tender no. 5476 went to LNER no. 2571 *Sunstar* in October 1940. *Trigo* went into Doncaster Works for a general repair in October 1940 and left with tender no. 5645 in November 1940. *Tracery* received no. 2571's GN type tender, no. 5281, when leaving Doncaster Works in December 1940 after a month undergoing a general repair. *Trigo* was at Neville Hill for fourteen years, leaving for Gateshead in December 1963, and was withdrawn from there a year later in November 1964.

Leeds 46161

Leeds Neville Hill shed was located on the eastern side of Leeds City Station and was built by the NER in 1894. The facility consisted of four roundhouses under one roof, later reduced to two by BR. It closed to steam in June 1966 to be used for diesel locomotives. LMS Royal Scot Class 4-6-0 locomotive no. 46161 *King's Own* entered service from Derby Works in September 1930. Based on the GWR 'Castle' Class there were seventy Royal Scot locomotives built between 1927 and 1930 to work the west coast main line. All of these were named predominantly after soldiers or regiments. *King's Own* is at Neville Hill in poor condition; it was withdrawn from Leeds Holbeck shed in December 1962.

Leeds 42152

Fairburn LMS Class 4P 2-6-4T locomotive no. 42152 was photographed at Leeds City Station. Opened in May 1938, the station was the result of the Wellington Station and New Station joining forces. Leeds Central Station services began operating from there in April 1967. No. 42152 was built at Derby Works in June 1948 and was one of 221 examples produced between 1945 and 1951 for use on suburban passenger trains. The engine spent the majority of its time allocated in the West Yorkshire area, working from such places as Mirfield, Manningham and Wakefield. At the time of the picture, no. 42152 was allocated to Holbeck shed where it only spent two months from July 1967. Withdrawal came in October from Low Moor shed.

Riccall 61419

Class B16 4-6-0 locomotive no. 61419 is working on the East Coast Main Line at Riccall. The engine was built at Darlington Works in November 1920 to Raven's S3 design for the NER. It originally carried a diagram 49 boiler, but this was replaced by a 49A diagram boiler in July 1947, which the locomotive carried for ten years until it too was replaced by an earlier type in May 1957. The diagram 49A boiler had a longer firebox, shorter barrel and the number of small tubes was increased to 156. If the diagram 49A boiler was fitted, the dome would be placed further back than it is here. No. 61419 left service in September 1961.

Riccall 61036

The East Coast Main Line no longer takes this route between Selby and York. The line now deviates at Temple Hirst Junction to the west and rejoins the old route at Colton Junction. This change was implemented in the early 1980s due to subsidence caused by mining in the area. The old track north of Selby was closed in 1989 and has been converted to a cycle track and a bypass. Thompson Class B1 4-6-0 locomotive no. 61036 *Ralph Assheton*, built in November 1947 at Darlington, was originally to be named 'Korrigum' as part of the Antelope series. This never materialised, and instead it was named after one of the final members of the LNER board. The engine was at Doncaster from December 1949 until withdrawal in September 1962; it was scrapped there in November.

York 69886

Seen here at York in a sorry state with peeling paint is a former NER Class D and LNER H1 Class 4-4-4T locomotive designed by V. Raven. No. 69886 was built at Darlington Works in September 1921 for use on local fast passenger services undertaking this work in the north-east during the 1920s and early 1930s. All forty-five members of the H1 Class were rebuilt by Gresley between 1931 and 1936 to a 4-6-2 wheel arrangement and were reclassified A8. No. 69886 was so treated in May 1936. After rebuilding, the type of trains the engines worked changed, becoming heavier and hauled over longer distances. The class found work on the east coast line and to the east coast from places like Leeds. The locomotive was withdrawn from Malton in June 1960 and scrapped at Darlington.

York 60847

Gresley Class V2 2-6-2 locomotive no. 60847 *St. Peter's School York A.D. 627* is seen at York. Built at Darlington in March 1939, the engine went to work at York. The allocation was only disturbed by a four-month period at Neville Hill, Leeds, from June 1946. No. 60847 is seen with separate cylinders, which were fitted in November 1961. This is identified from the steam pipe connecting to the cylinder from the smokebox. Originally it was part of one unit that comprised the smokebox saddle and cylinders, however, these were prone to failures and the front end was redesigned to make repairs easier. No. 60847 was withdrawn in September 1965.

York 60152

Peppercorn Class A1 Pacific no. 60152 *Holyrood* was the last of the class to be built at Darlington in July 1949. Its first allocation was to Edinburgh Haymarket shed, followed by Polmadie where it had a couple of spells in the early 1950s, returning to Haymarket each time. *Holyrood* arrived at York in September 1964 after a year at St Margaret's and ten years at Haymarket. When the A1s were introduced, York was given five engines to run services to Newcastle and it was not until later on that they were scheduled to run further afield. Thirteen A1s had reached York by the start of 1964 as diesel engines had displaced them from sheds in the south. No. 60152 was withdrawn in June 1965.

York 92206

BR Standard Class 9F 2-10-0 locomotive no. 92206 entered traffic from Swindon Works in May 1959. The 9F Class was designed by R. A. Riddles for working heavy freight trains and 251 examples were produced between 1954 and 1960 at Swindon and Crewe. No. 92206 was first allocated to the BR western region before it went on loan to the southern region. The engine arrived at York in September 1963, staying over three years before its reallocation to Wakefield and subsequent withdrawal from there in May 1967. From York the engine could find itself in the North East, around Hull or in the Manchester area. No. 92206 has BR1G tender no. 1542, which had a capacity of 5,000 gallons and 7 tons of coal. The sides do not extend all the way to the top as on other tenders; this was a measure introduced to allow better vision when the engine was running tender first.

York 69008

The J72 0-6-0T locomotive was designed by Wilson Worsdell for the NER. Seventy-five were built and classified E1. The LNER added ten to their ranks with BR contributing a further twenty-eight. No. 69008, seen at York south shed, was built by BR at Darlington in December 1949. The BR engines only differed slightly from those built earlier, the changes bringing them up to modern standards. The locomotive was resident at York from February 1960 to October 1961 and withdrawn from Gateshead in December 1963.

York 41252

The LMS Class 2 2-6-2T locomotives were designed by H. G. Ivatt and built by Crewe and Derby Works between 1946 and 1952, giving a total of 130. No. 41252 was erected at Crewe in November 1949 and was in service for thirteen years before withdrawal in December 1962. The locomotive was only resident at York for two months during the late 1950s; it arrived from Malton in April 1959 and left for Neville Hill in June.

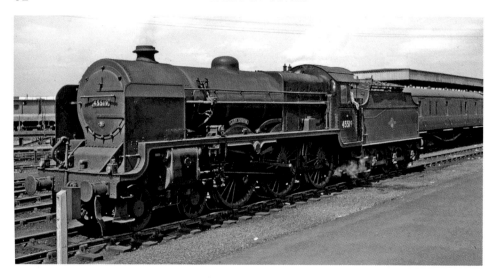

York 45519

The first station to serve York was a temporary terminus built by the York & North Midland Railway in May 1839. It opened after the first phase of the York to Normanton line was completed; the first part of the track went as far as Milford, with the connection to Normanton being completed a year later. LMS Fowler 'Patriot' Class 4-6-0 locomotive no. 45519 *Lady Godiva*, was built at Crewe Works in February 1933 and had a twenty-nine-year career before its withdrawal in March 1962. The engine was Bristol-based at the time of the picture so a long journey home was in store. It was at Bristol Barrow Road shed for four years from November 1958, but for the previous ten years it had spent the majority of its time at Preston, Carlisle, Crewe and Longsight.

York 60102

Seen here at York is the second of the Gresley A1 Class Pacifics to be built. No. 60102 *Sir Frederick Banbury*, LNER no. 4471, GNR no. 1471, was constructed at Doncaster in July 1922. Its first allocation was a ten-year spell at Doncaster, however, its first four months were spent on loan to King's Cross shed working services to Peterborough and back. It was rebuilt to A3 in October 1942 and received a double chimney in April 1959. It is seen with GNR type tender no. 5292, which it carried after being rebuilt. No. 60102 was one of six to be withdrawn in 1961, leaving service in November.

York 68431

In the derelict York south no. 3 shed is Class J77 0-6-0T locomotive no. 68431. The building was constructed by the NER during 1864 and was later let to the Midland Railway before they moved to the old works building, known as Queen Street shed. The roof was left to deteriorate to such an extent that it had to be removed, but the space continued to be utilised until its closure in May 1961. No. 68431 was originally built as NER Class G6 in 1879 at Gateshead, but was rebuilt to NER Class 290, by W. Worsdell at York in December 1900. The engine was withdrawn in February 1960.

York 65698

Class J25 0-6-0 engine no. 65698 was formerly a part of the NER P1 Class and is seen here outside York south no. 3 shed. It entered service from Gateshead in May 1900. During the Second World War the locomotive was among forty loaned to the Great Western Railway, lasting from November 1939 until January 1946. York was the locomotive's final allocation, arriving in June 1958; it was withdrawn in September 1959.

York 61428

Six engine sheds were utilised at York south; three roundhouses and three straight sheds. Only two roundhouses and a straight shed survived to see the end of steam allocations at York south in 1961. The straight shed was built by the Great North of England Railway in 1841; after Grouping it housed LMS engines until Nationalisation. Behind the locomotive is York south no. 2 shed, which also survived and was built by the Y&NMR in 1852; the other was York no. 3 shed. The site was subsequently cleared and the roundhouses were demolished around 1963. Class B16 4-6-0 locomotive no. 61428 was built at Darlington in March 1921. It had a thirty-nine-year career before withdrawal in October 1960.

York 60526

The second station was opened at York in January 1841 by the Y&NM and the Great North of England Railway (later NER), who were in the process of completing a line to Darlington and then Gateshead. This station was in use until its replacement by the present station, which is situated to the west of the second station. It was opened in June 1877 by the NER to a curved pattern with thirteen platforms. Peppercorn Class A2 4-6-2 locomotive no. 60526 *Sugar Palm* was built at Doncaster Works in January 1948, receiving a double chimney in October 1949. The engine was one of five fitted with M.L.S. multiple valve regulators, with the operating rod visible above the boiler handrail. *Sugar Palm* was a long-term York resident, being allocated from September 1948 until withdrawn in November 1962.

CHAPTER 4

Harrogate to Blyth

Harrogate 90054

War Department 'Austerity' Class 2-8-0 no. 90054 is seen here entering Harrogate Starbeck shed. At either side are two Gresley Class J39 0-6-0 locomotives, numbers 64942 and 64944. No. 90054 was built at the North British Locomotive Co. in April 1944. It was on loan to the LNER after returning from Europe in November 1945 and later purchased by the company for £4,500 along with 200 others. The locomotive was allocated to Newport, which had a large allocation of the class in the post-war years, followed by moves to Consett and Tyne Dock in the mid-1950s. It arrived at Starbeck in June 1957 and spent two years there before moving to Wakefield in September 1959. The J39s were long-term residents at Starbeck, but both were also moved in September 1959. No. 90054 was withdrawn from Normanton in January 1967.

Harrogate 62759

A total of seventy-six D49 locomotives were built; they were split into three sub-classes. Forty-two engines comprised class part two; these had Lentz poppet valves operated by a rotary cam. The class were either named after counties, mostly with the suffix 'shire', or hunts. Gresley Class D49 4-4-0 locomotive no. 62759 *The Craven* was built at Darlington in August 1934 and fell into part two of the class. The Craven hunt took place in the Hungerford and Newbury areas of Berkshire. No. 62759 is seen at Starbeck shed where it was allocated from December 1954. It was reallocated to Hull Dairycoates in September 1959 and withdrawn in January 1961.

Harrogate 42477

Starbeck shed was built by the NER to the south of Starbeck Station, Harrogate, in 1857 as a two-track through shed. It was extended four times by the company between 1865, and 1889 and was later rebuilt by BR in 1956. The shed only lasted a further three years before closure by BR in September 1959; it was demolished in around 1962. Commercial premises and a housing development now occupy the site. LMS Stanier Class 4P 2-6-2T locomotive no. 42477 was built at Derby Works in January 1937. It was allocated to Starbeck for five months in January 1959 and moved to York. Withdrawal came in June 1965 from Chester.

Harrogate 64847

Class J39 0-6-0 locomotives were originally put into sub-classes according to the type of tenders that they carried. No. 64847, built at Darlington in May 1933, was in class part one, as it carried the 3,500-gallon tender. It has straight sides, whereas earlier engines carrying the same tender had stepped-out sides. The locomotive was allocated to Heaton when new and went to Starbeck in September 1953 after spells at Darlington and Middlesbrough. A move to Selby followed in June 1959 then to York in September. It was withdrawn in September 1962 from Sunderland.

Harrogate 62763

Class D49 4-4-0 locomotive no. 62763 *The Fitzwilliam*, pictured at Harrogate Starbeck shed, was built at Darlington in September 1934 in class part two. The locomotive is seen here with a group standard tender which has a 4,200-gallon water capacity and space for over 7 tons of coal. The original livery for the D49s was LNER green with black and white lining. During the War this changed to black and at Nationalisation it stayed that way, with only the addition of grey, red and cream lining. The locomotive was withdrawn in January 1961 with the last of the class going in May. No. 62712 *Morayshire* was preserved and is currently at the Bo'ness and Kinneil Railway operated by the Scottish Railway Preservation Society.

Scarborough 62739

Scarborough Londesborough Road Station was opened by the NER in June 1908 as Washbeck Excursion Station; its purpose was to relieve the pressure brought on Scarborough Station during holiday periods. On 1 June 1933 the station's name was changed to Scarborough Londesborough Road, and at the same time it also became a public station. It closed in August 1963 with the excursion services transferred to Scarborough Station, but the site was still used for storing the excursion coaching stock. Final closure came in July 1966 and the site has subsequently been used as commercial premises. Gresley Class D49 4-4-0 locomotive no. 62739 *The Badsworth* is pictured at Scarborough Londesborough Road Station.

Scarborough 62739

The Badsworth was built at Darlington in May 1932 in class part two. The locomotive was one of fifteen in this section of the class to receive tenders from the J38s. In turn, the latter received tenders originally intended for the D49s. In November 1955 the tender was changed for a N.E. type, originally from a part three locomotive, which had in turn come from a Q6 Class engine. A further exchange occurred in May 1958 when it was attached to a G.C. type tender, which had previously been with an engine from class part one. These tenders were rebuilt in the late 1940s to have straight sides, replacing the original stepped-out sides. *The Badsworth* was at Scarborough shed from July 1951 until its withdrawal in October 1960.

Darlington 61757

Gresley Class K2 2-6-0 locomotive no. 61757 was built at the North British Locomotive Company's Hyde Park Works in August 1918. The order for the twenty engines built by the NBLC was initially given to Beyer, Peacock & Co. in 1915. However, the Ministry of Munitions stopped the production. A compromise was reached and the construction work and materials were transferred to NBLC in November 1917. The locomotive's first allocation was King's Cross where it spent the first ten years of its time in service. It also worked in East Anglia moving between sheds in that region and also saw a few extended allocations to March shed. Withdrawal came from Boston in February 1959; it is pictured here at Darlington awaiting the cutting torch.

Darlington 68047

Class J94 0-6-0ST locomotive no. 68047, was photographed at Darlington shed in front of the mechanical coaler. The locomotive was built by W. G. Bagnall & Co. in July 1945 to the designs of R. A. Riddles, becoming WD no. 75258 and then LNER 8047. The construction work had been sub-contracted by the Hunslet Engine Company. As BR no. 68047, the engine, a long-term Darlington resident, was withdrawn from the shed in May 1965.

Darlington 62003

The North British Locomotive Co. built Peppercorn Class K1 2-6-0 locomotive no. 62003 in June 1949, entering service at Darlington shed. From there, the engine moved to Heaton, working goods trains to Edinburgh, and then returned to Darlington in July 1952 for a six-year stay. No. 62003 found further work at sheds in the North East during the late 1950s and early 1960s, when it spent three years at Northallerton working to places such as York, Thirsk, Darlington and Newport. Its last allocation was a return to Darlington in March 1963; it was withdrawn in June 1965.

Darlington 69842

Class A5 4-6-2T locomotive no. 69842 was the last of the class to be constructed in March 1926; the builder was Hawthorn Leslie & Co., who was responsible for thirteen locos. As the engine was built after Grouping, it featured alterations made by the LNER to the original design. These included modifying the exterior so that it conformed to the rolling stock gauge, and the cylinders were also altered with the piston diameter reduced in size. The locomotive was allocated to Blaydon when new, and then moved to Saltburn and Darlington where it worked the service between the two locations. Although built to work in the North East, the engine spent time in the south at Norwich, Neasden and Stratford. It was withdrawn from Thornaby in October 1958 and is photographed in Darlington scrap yard.

Darlington 65784

Class J27 0-6-0 locomotive no. 65784 is seen here at Darlington sidings, hauling a coal train. The engine was built at Darlington Works in May 1906 as a member of NER Class P3, designed by W. Worsdell; by 1923 the total number reached 115. As NER 880, it was erected with a saturated boiler and slide valves whereas the later engines built in the 1920s had superheated boilers and piston valves. In 1937 the design of the boiler was modified and classified diagram 57A. No. 65784 carried this type of boiler from June 1946 until it was withdrawn in August 1959. The locomotive was allocated to Percy Main shed at the time it left service; this was an area where many J27s could be found when not hauling coal trains around the North East, which was their main duty.

Darlington 61274

One of the crew balancing dangerously on coals on top of the tender suggests this picture of Thompson Class B1 4-6-0 no. 61274 was taken at a time when health and safety was an afterthought. Nevertheless, the picture shows water being taken on to the group standard tender, which had a 4,200-gallon water capacity. The tender was constructed by welding, with a variety existing that were riveted, and this tender has the second BR emblem that is facing the wrong way. The engine was built by the North British Locomotive Co. in January 1948 and entered service at Darlington. It had spells in the south and at York during the 1950s, returning both times to Darlington, finally leaving in June 1959 for Low Moor shed. It was withdrawn from Wakefield in November 1964.

Darlington 69006

A view at the north-east end of Darlington shed. In the foreground is Class J72 0-6-0T locomotive no. 69006 built at Darlington Works in November 1949. Further along from no. 69006 is Class J21 0-6-0 locomotive no. 65117 built at Gateshead Works in April 1894. The engine entered service as NER Class C1, which had simple expansion cylinders. The other locomotives, NER Class C, had compound expansion cylinders, however, these were altered to the C1 cylinder type. No. 65117 was withdrawn in February 1959 and scrapped at Darlington, while no. 69006 survived until December 1963, when it was withdrawn from Darlington shed.

Darlington 68007

Class J94 0-6-0ST locomotive no. 68007 was built by Hudswell, Clarke & Co. in February 1944. A total of 377 locomotives were built for the War Department to the design, which was based on the Hunslet 50550 Class. After the War some locomotives were sold to industry, others were bought by railway companies in Holland and ninety were kept to work for the armed forces. Both the LNER and BR made slight modifications to the engines; one seen here is the central extension to the coal bunker, which reaches the top of the cab. This was added to no. 68007 in November 1949. The locomotive was allocated to Darlington in November 1956 and it is seen here in the works yard. The engine was resident at the shed until withdrawn in October 1962.

Darlington 60533

Darlington Station, also known as Darlington Bank Top, was opened by the Great North of England Railway during March 1841 after the completion of the line to York. The station was rebuilt in 1860 and again in the 1880s. The result of the last rebuild by the NER was the present station, which was opened in July 1887. Peppercorn Class A2 4-6-2 locomotive no. 60533 *Happy Knight* is seen here at Darlington Station; it was built at Doncaster Works in April 1948. The engine was fitted with a double chimney in December 1949 and at the same time received a M.L.S. multi-valve regulator. A total of six engines in the class received double chimneys. Withdrawal from service came in June 1963 while at New England shed.

Darlington 60004

Class A4 4-6-2 locomotive no. 60004 *William Whitelaw* is pictured at Darlington in June 1965. The locomotive entered Darlington Works on 5 July 1965 for casual light repairs and left on 28 August. Doncaster was the usual works responsible for repairs to the class but this had ceased by 1963. *William Whitelaw* had only one previous visit to Darlington Works, where it had undergone casual heavy repairs between December 1963 and February 1964. The engine had visited Cowlairs and Inverurie Works during its time in service in Scotland. After withdrawal the locomotive was sold for scrap to Motherwell Machinery and Scrap; the deed had been done by October 1966.

Darlington 63460

Class Q7 0-8-0 locomotive no. 63460 was originally built for the NER and designed by V. Raven as a Class T3 locomotive. It was the first of the class to emerge from Darlington Works in October 1919 as NER no. 901. Five were built by the NER and ten were added by the LNER. The class was somewhat nomadic during the early years but all the locomotives were allocated to Tyne Dock in March 1943 and put to work on heavy mineral traffic at the Consett steelworks. Withdrawal for no. 63460 came in December 1962 and it is seen here at Darlington being stored waiting for preservation. The locomotive is currently in residence at Darlington's Head of Steam Museum.

Darlington 60919

Darlington-built Class V2 2-6-2 locomotive no. 60919 in September 1941. It entered service at Heaton, spending the next four years in the North East at Gateshead and Tweedmouth. In October 1945 it was transferred north of the border to Scotland and worked nineteen years at Aberdeen. From there the locomotive could be put to work on a number of duties including express passenger/ goods, and the express fish services to Edinburgh. From the late 1940s the V2s at Aberdeen saw their scope of operation increase to Perth, Glasgow, Carstairs and Carlisle. The vast majority of the servicing on this locomotive was performed by Darlington Works with visits to Doncaster in 1945 and Inverurie in 1951. No. 60919 left service from Dundee in September 1966 and was scrapped by Arnott Young.

Darlington 62008

Seen heading towards the shed is long-term Darlington resident Peppercorn Class K1 2-6-0 locomotive no. 62008. It was built by the North British Locomotive Co. in June 1949 and was allocated to Darlington. From there it would have worked medium distance goods trains around the North East and to York. The locomotive is equipped with a group standard tender, which in the mid-1950s was modified to have the coal division plate placed further forward to keep coal away from the filling hole for the water tank. No. 62008's only other allocation was to West Hartlepool in March 1966 where it spent nine months before leaving service in December 1966.

Darlington 60036

Pictured at the turntable at Darlington shed is Gresley A3 Pacific no. 60036 *Colombo*. Built in July 1934 at Doncaster Works, the locomotive arrived at Darlington in December 1963 after periods at Gateshead, York, Heaton, King's Cross, Neville Hill, Copley Hill and Ardsley. The shed, seen behind the locomotive, was built by the LNER in 1940 and consisted of several roads open at both ends. This replaced an earlier facility located on the same site, which had been put in use by the NER in 1885. It had five through tracks and four dead end tracks. *Colombo* was withdrawn in November 1964.

Darlington 12119

British Rail Class 11 diesel shunting locomotive no. 12119 was built by Darlington Works in September 1952 and started its service at Hull Dairycoates. The design for the locomotive was based on a type produced by the LMS and a total of 106 were built between 1948 and 1952. Darlington produced thirty-six, with the others built at Derby Works, and they were equipped with English Electric Co. engines. No. 12119, seen here at Darlington, was withdrawn in November 1968. It was scrapped by NCB Philadelphia in November 1985.

Thornaby 63399

Class Q6 0-8-0 locomotive no. 63399 was built at Darlington in December 1918. The engine was originally attached to a self-trimming tender but in February 1935, in the tender exchange with the C7 Class, it received a tender from no. 722. No. 63399 was allocated to Thornaby shed between November 1959 and December 1962. It arrived from Blaydon and left for Tyne Dock. Thornaby had a large allocation of Q6s as it absorbed the allocations of Middlesbrough, Stockton, Haverton Hill and Newport when those sheds closed. From Thornaby the class worked goods and mineral traffic throughout the North East and to York and Leeds. No. 63399 was withdrawn in March 1964.

Thornaby 65756

Thornaby shed was built in 1958 by British Railways to the east of the railway station with the same name. The motive behind building the shed was to replace the sheds in the area which were many years out of date and in desperate need of renovation. Two buildings were built to house the locomotives; one was a roundhouse and the other was a thirteen-track straight shed. Class J26 0-6-0 locomotive no. 65756 entered traffic from Gateshead in May 1905. Allocation to Thornaby came in June 1958 when Newport shed closed. The engine was withdrawn in June 1962 from the former shed. December 1964 saw Thornaby's allocation switch from steam to diesel locomotives and the shed remained in use until around 2008 when it was closed. Demolition occurred in 2011.

West Hartlepool 63395

Seen at Hartlepool is no. 63395, a Raven-designed Class Q6 0-8-0 engine. It was built at Darlington Works in December 1918. Upon Nationalisation the locomotive was allocated at West Hartlepool, moving to Selby in December 1949. The locomotive was one of three to be withdrawn in September 1967 bringing the service life of the class to an end. No. 63395 was subsequently preserved by the North Eastern Locomotive Preservation Group. It was housed at Hartlepool for five months between October 1968 and February 1969 for refurbishment work.

Sunderland 69883

Two Class A8 4-6-2T locomotives, nos. 69883 and 69853 are featured here at Sunderland South Dock shed. Both engines were built at Darlington Works; no. 69883 in August 1921 and no. 69853 in November 1913. They were later rebuilt from LNER Class H1 to A8 by Gresley in August 1934 and May 1935 respectively. The shed comprised two dead end tracks, built by the NER in 1857, with a similar facility added in 1861 and a roundhouse built in 1875. The shed was closed to steam allocations in September 1967. The straight sheds saw further use as a diesel depot but the roundhouse was demolished. Final closure came in the late 1980s and demolition of the rest of the facilities followed in 1990. No. 69883 was withdrawn from Sunderland in June 1960, while no. 69853 went slightly earlier in January. Both were scrapped at Darlington.

Gateshead 69109

The picture shows a NER Class U 0-6-2T engine, which later became LNER Class N10. As NER no. 1716 it was the last of the twenty-strong class to enter service in April 1903. All were built at Darlington to the design of Wilson Worsdell. No. 69109 (from July 1948) was a long-term Gateshead resident; it was withdrawn from there in April 1962. A total of seven roundhouses were built to serve Gateshead shed, along with two straight sheds. By the early 1900s, three of the roundhouses had been closed and utilised by Gateshead Works. Four roundhouses and two straight sheds were used at Gateshead until it closed to steam in March 1965.

Gateshead 60001

After closure to steam, Gateshead shed was converted to a diesel depot and two roundhouses were rebuilt as straight sheds which were open at each end. Final closure came in July 1991 and the site has subsequently become a housing estate. This Class A4 Pacific was built at Doncaster Works in April 1938 and entered service as LNER no. 4500 *Garganey*. It only carried this name for a short time, becoming *Sir Ronald Matthews* in March 1939 after the LNER Chairman. Gateshead was the locomotive's only shed, and it was withdrawn from there in October 1964.

Pelaw Junction 63371

Photographed at Pelaw Junction in June 1959 is a Q6 Class 0-8-0 locomotive. Pelaw Junction is located to the east of Newcastle and Gateshead and was once part of the East Coast Main Line until a new route was developed in 1872. The junction is where the line from Newcastle and Gateshead parts to South Shields, the Durham Coast Line and the old Leamside Line branch. No. 63371 was built in May 1917 at Darlington and is attached to the original-type self-trimming tender. The engine was withdrawn from Tyne Dock in November 1965.

Pelaw Junction 63377

Class Q6 0-8-0 locomotive no. 63377 is pictured at Pelaw Junction in June 1959, working on a mineral train. The engine was built at Darlington in June 1917 with a diagram 50 boiler. The diameter of the boiler was 5 feet 6 inches and 15 feet 7.5 inches long with a firebox heating surface of 140 square feet. In September 1949 the locomotive was fitted with a diagram 50A boiler, which had an improved firebox heating service to 145 square feet. The engine carried this type of boiler until it left service from Tyne Dock in November 1966.

South Blyth 65862

Seen at South Blyth shed is Class J27 0-6-0 locomotive no. 65862, built by Darlington Works in December 1921 for the NER. The engine differed to earlier members of the class as it featured a superheated boiler and piston valves instead of slide valves; thirty-five members of the class were built with these differences. These locomotives were also fitted with a different style tender with oval frame slots between the wheels. However, the locomotive is fitted with an earlier type tender as the frame slots are of a former pattern. The superheater was removed from the locomotive in July 1945 and at the same time it received a diagram 50A boiler. No. 65862 left service in October 1965.

South Blyth 65727

Class J25 0-6-0 locomotive no. 65727, at South Blyth shed, was built at Gateshead in November 1902. The engine is attached to a 3,038-gallon tender with a coal capacity of 5 tons. Before being replaced by larger locomotives, the J25s were used on mineral and goods traffic. No. 65727 (as LNER 2142) was loaned to the GWR between February 1940 and November 1946. In BR days the locomotive was allocated to South Blyth from April 1955 until January 1961, at which time the engine left service.

South Blyth 65822

South Blyth shed was located west of Blyth Station and was built by the NER in 1880. The structure consisted of three tracks with dead ends. In 1894 three more tracks were added and other facilities were upgraded. The shed was closed by BR during May 1967 and demolished around 1970. Class J27 0-6-0 locomotive no. 65822 was built by the North British Locomotive Co. in June 1908. The locomotive was a long-time resident at South Blyth shed in its later years, arriving from Percy Main in July 1951. It was condemned while at the shed fourteen years later in March 1965.

CHAPTER 5

Edinburgh Portobello
to Aberdeen Kittybrewster

Edinburgh Portobello 65224
Pictured at Portobello sidings, Edinburgh, is Class J36 0-6-0 locomotive no. 65224 *Mons*. It was built for the North British Railway at Cowlairs Works in February 1891. During the First World War some of the class were posted to Europe with the ROD. On return, these locomotives were named after important events or people associated with the conflict. *Mons* takes its name from the Belgian town where the British Army fought the first battle of the conflict. The locomotive was allocated to St Margaret's shed at the time of the photograph and had a long allocation there. It was withdrawn in May 1963 after seventy-two years' service.

Edinburgh Portobello 64482

Portobello sidings are located to the east of Edinburgh Waverley Station between Joppa and Craigentinny; Portobello Junction is where the East Coast Main Line meets the suburban line for Edinburgh. The locomotive was built at Cowlairs Works in December 1908 to the designs of W. P. Reid. It was part of NBR Class B, intended for goods services. The class eventually totalled seventy-six and became LNER Class J35. No. 64482 is also a St Margaret's engine but it had a shorter allocation lasting only two years from March 1959 until its withdrawal in June 1961.

Edinburgh St Margaret's 65934

This image was taken at St Margaret's shed, Edinburgh, and captures Gresley Class J38 0-6-0 locomotive no. 65934. Built in May 1926, the engine was the last of the class to be built. Construction had started in January at Darlington; the class eventually numbering thirty-five. All of the locomotives were based in Scotland and they worked on goods, mineral and passenger services. No. 65934 was originally paired with a group standard tender with stepped-out sides, however, this was taken for use on either an O2, D49 or J39 Class locomotive during September 1933. No. 65934 is seen with a straight-sided 3,500-gallon tender, which also has the second BR emblem applied the wrong way round and so does the tender on the right. No. 65934 was withdrawn in December 1966.

Edinburgh St Margaret's 68472

An illustration of the changing times at St Margaret's shed. Class J83 0-6-0T locomotive no. 68472 is seen alongside Class 08 diesel shunting locomotive that was allocated to the shed in 1959. No. 68472 was one of forty built for the NBR between 1900 and 1901. It was erected by Sharp, Stewart & Co. in April 1901 to the designs of M. Holmes for use on short-distance services and heavy shunting. The locomotives were rebuilt with a new boiler and had other modifications made by the LNER between 1924 and 1925. No. 68472 underwent these alterations in October 1924. It was withdrawn from St Margaret's shed in February 1962.

Edinburgh St Margaret's 69150

This N15/1 Class 0-6-2T locomotive entered traffic from the North British Locomotive Co.'s Queens Park Works in August 1912. When new it formed part of the NBR's Class A, which by Grouping totalled seventy-five engines. Thirty more were added by the LNER, who classified the locomotives into three categories according to certain aspects of their design. Six went into Class N14, while the N15 Class was split into two sub-classes N15/1(93) and N15/2 (6). The N15/1 engines had longer cabs and steam or vacuum brakes, which differentiated them from the other two class parts. No. 69150 arrived at St Margaret's from Dundee Tay Bridge in May 1958, and was withdrawn from the former in October 1962.

Edinburgh St Margaret's 61007

Thompson Class B1 4-6-0 locomotive no. 61007 *Klipspringer* is pictured at St Margaret's shed which was located to the east of Waverley Station and at one time it had the largest allocation of any shed in the city; 221 locomotives. The first shed on the site was a roundhouse built by the NBR in 1846. In 1866, to the south-east of the first shed, a six-track straight shed was built, again by the NBR. 1871 saw a square roundhouse added to the site by the NBR for use by the NER, who used it for only thirty years before it was handed over to the NBR. No. 61007 was built at Darlington in April 1944 and after spending a brief period allocated there, it spent the rest of its career in Scotland. Haymarket was the principle shed, with only a month at Dundee in the late 1940s breaking up its sixteen-year stay. Moves to Dalry Road, St Margaret's (October 1961 to December 1962), Eastfield and Ayr followed with withdrawal coming from the latter in February 1964.

Edinburgh St Margaret's 68342

Seen to the left of the locomotive, where 68472 is located, was the site of the first roundhouse built at St Margaret's. The building was destroyed by a fire in the early 1940s and was subsequently demolished. However, the tracks remained in situ for the stabling of the shed's tank engines and later the diesel shunting locomotives. It was used in this way until the shed closed in May 1967; the site has since been cleared. The Class J88 0-6-0 locomotive seen in the image was built at Cowlairs Works during May 1912 for light shunting duties. It fulfilled this role for close to fifty years until it left service in February 1962.

Edinburgh Haymarket 68454

Located to the west of Edinburgh Waverley Station on the Edinburgh-Glasgow line, this shed would have been hard to miss due to the bright-coloured distemper used. Class J83 0-6-0T locomotive no. 68454 was built by Neilson, Reid & Co. in March 1901, one of twenty built by the company. It was rebuilt by the LNER in November 1924; apart from the change in boiler, modifications included Ross pop safety valves fitted to the rear of the boiler, helical springs replacing laminated springs and larger sandboxes. The locomotive left service in February 1962 with the last of the class going in December.

Edinburgh Haymarket 60160

Waiting for a signal allowing it on to the Edinburgh-Glasgow line is Peppercorn Class A1 Pacific no. 60160 *Auld Reekie*. Doncaster Works built the engine in December 1949 and its first allocation was Haymarket. From there the locomotive hauled express passenger services on the main lines, but rarely went further south than Newcastle. In the early 1950s the locomotive had two spells at Polmadie shed, Glasgow, where it would have worked services to Carlisle, Crewe and Edinburgh. *Auld Reekie* returned to Haymarket in February 1952 and was allocated to the shed for the next eleven years. It had three months at St Margaret's in September 1963 and left service from there at the end of the year.

BR Steam in Colour

Edinburgh Haymarket 60147

Visiting Edinburgh Haymarket shed is Peppercorn A1 no. 60147 *North Eastern*, a Gateshead resident. The locomotive entered traffic from Darlington Works in April 1949 and its first allocation was the latter shed. The locomotive was named after the North Eastern Railway, which was one of the companies amalgamated to form the LNER. Three other locomotives carried names in recognition of this. *North Eastern* received its nameplates in March 1952 and carried the hand-painted coats of arms of the constituent company; as did the other three. No. 60147 had spells at Heaton and Tweedmouth before withdrawn from York in August 1964.

Edinburgh Haymarket 61025

Thompson Class B1 4-6-0 locomotive no. 61025 *Pallah* is another 'foreigner' at Edinburgh Haymarket shed, although it was once briefly a resident there. The engine was built at Darlington Works in April 1947 and allocated to Tweedmouth. Between August and October 1948, *Pallah* was a Haymarket resident, returning to Tweedmouth where it spent twelve years and was allocated to at the time of the picture. Further moves to Blaydon and Alnmouth followed before it was withdrawn in December 1962 and scrapped at Darlington. A total of 40 B1s were named after breeds of antelope, with Pallah being the name of the Impala in Bantu, an African language.

Edinburgh Haymarket 60095

The locomotive is pictured at the north-east end of the shed with the mechanical coaler seen just above the roof. The first Haymarket shed was located at Haymarket Railway Station and was built in 1842 by the Edinburgh & Glasgow Railway. The building was made of stone and had two tracks. Class A3 4-6-2 locomotive no. 60095 *Flamingo* was built as an A3 at Doncaster during February 1929; after running in there it was allocated to Carlisle, which (including 60095) saw three new A3s arrive during 1929. These locomotives worked three return services a day on the Edinburgh Waverley to Carlisle portion for trains bound for either London St Pancras or Leeds. *Flamingo* spent the rest of its life in service at Carlisle and was withdrawn from there in April 1961 to be scrapped at Doncaster.

Edinburgh Haymarket 60009

Another view at the north-east end of the shed, this time featuring Haymarket resident no. 60009 *Union of South Africa*. The locomotive was built at Doncaster in June 1937 as LNER no. 4488 *Osprey*. However, this name only lasted while the locomotive was in Doncaster Works paint shop undergoing trials with a new paint scheme. When entering traffic the name had become *Union of South Africa*; *Osprey* was subsequently allocated to LNER no. 4494 (later BR no. 60003 *Andrew K. McCosh*). The locomotive is seen with the South African coat of arms on the cab and a plaque of a Springbok on the boiler casing. The latter was attached in April 1954 after being donated for use. No. 60009 was withdrawn from Aberdeen in June 1966 and has been preserved.

Edinburgh Haymarket 60005
As LNER no. 4901 *Capercaillie*, the locomotive entered traffic from Doncaster Works in June 1938. Its only allocation for the first twenty-five years in service was to Gateshead. During that time the locomotive was renamed twice; first to *Charles H. Newton* in August 1942 and then *Sir Charles Newton* in June 1943. This gentleman was the Chief General Manager of the LNER and the change of name acknowledged his knighthood. No. 60005 (from July 1948) moved to St Margaret's in October 1963 and again, in November, to Aberdeen. Unlike other members of the class it did not find a new lease of life on the Aberdeen to Glasgow expresses. It left service in March 1964 and was sold for scrap.

Edinburgh Haymarket 60038
Gresley 4-6-2 locomotive no. 60038 *Firdaussi* was built to A3 specifications at Doncaster in August 1934. The Edinburgh Haymarket shed turntable – 70 feet in length – was constructed by Ransomes & Rapier. It was installed about 1931 and was originally manually operated. After the War a vacuum motor was fitted and this operated from the engine's vacuum brake pipe as seen here. A 50-foot turntable had originally been installed when the shed was built, but this became too small and the larger engines had to be turned by running around the local lines. *Firdaussi* spent much of its time allocated to sheds in the North East, but during the early 1960s it was at Holbeck and Neville Hill until withdrawal came in November 1963.

Edinburgh Haymarket 60537

Peppercorn Class A2 4-6-2 locomotive no. 60537 *Bachelors Button*, seen on the Haymarket shed turntable, was built at Doncaster during June 1948. After initial allocations to Copley Hill and New England the locomotive was moved to Aberdeen. However, while at the latter shed it was noted as being a poor performer, which was later accredited to a chimney and blastpipe problem. An exchange occurred with 60532 *Blue Peter* and no. 60537 took its place at Haymarket and spent the next ten years there. *Bachelors Button* was withdrawn from St Margaret's in December 1962.

Edinburgh Haymarket 68320

This locomotive was the first of NBR Class F to be built in December 1904. Cowlairs Works was responsible for erecting all thirty-five members of the class, the last one leaving there in 1919. In May 1925, as LNER no. 9836, the locomotive was rebuilt with a new boiler and the safety valves were moved to the rear of the boiler. The engine was built with a wooden buffer beam, seen here, and had shorter buffers that were later changed to conform to the rest of the class. One area in which it remained different was the number of coal rails; it has two whereas later members of the class had four. Removal from service came in June 1960.

Edinburgh Haymarket 60509

The design for the Thompson Class A2/1 4-6-2 locomotives took elements from the A2/2 Class (rebuilt P2s) and Gresley V2s. All four members of the class were built at Darlington between May 1944 and January 1945 and were constructed instead of four V2 Class locomotives. No. 60509 *Waverley*, as LNER no. 3698, entered service in November 1944 and was initially allocated to Darlington. It arrived for duties at Haymarket in March 1945 and spent fifteen years there, broken only by a few weeks at Aberdeen in September 1949. Its duties from Haymarket included express passenger services on the main routes and also express goods. In May 1960 it broke cylinder bolts and was subsequently withdrawn in August. The engine was scrapped at Doncaster; a fate which also befell the rest of the class.

Edinburgh Haymarket 62709

Gresley Class D49 4-4-0 locomotive no. 62709 *Berwickshire* was built at Darlington in January 1928 in class part one, indicating it has piston valves fitted. Twenty-eight members of the class were built with this arrangement and six were modified later. This happened when engines falling into part three of the class had their oscillating cam valve gear replaced. No. 62709 is attached to a G.C.-type tender with curved sides; it received this one in January 1942. The locomotive was a long-time Haymarket resident, and was withdrawn from there in January 1960.

Edinburgh Haymarket 60535

Seen in immaculate condition outside the fitting shed at Haymarket is Peppercorn Class A2 Pacific no. 60535 *Hornets Beauty*. This shed was added to the facilities just after the end of the War; it was located at the north end of the building, adding a further two roads, which could be accessed from both ends. *Hornets Beauty* was erected at Doncaster in May 1948, and after eighteen months at York arrived at Haymarket. A total of six of the class had found their way to the shed by 1951 and all stayed until a mass departure between October and November 1961. No. 60535 saw further service at St Margaret's and Polmadie, and was dispensed with in June 1965.

Edinburgh Haymarket 62685

At the west side of the shed is Class D11 4-4-0 locomotive no. 62685 *Malcolm Graeme*, built by Armstrong Whitworth & Co. in October 1924 in class part two. The first part of the class included the locomotives built earlier, which formed GCR Class 11F, designed by J. Robinson. Twenty-Four locomotives were built by the LNER after Grouping and the differences between the two class parts only consisted of minor details. Allocation to Haymarket for no. 62685 came after its first allocation to St Margaret's and it spent the rest of the time in service at the former shed. Towards the end of its career, no. 62685 was used as a stationary boiler at Haymarket and then for the Caledonian Hotel. Withdrawal came in January 1962.

Edinburgh Haymarket 62719
Seen to the left of the locomotive is Jeffrey's Brewery, one of many breweries in the area surrounding Haymarket shed. Gresley Class D49/1 4-4-0 locomotive no. 62719 *Peebles-shire* was built at Darlington in May 1928. It was a long-term resident at Haymarket, arriving in March 1943 and staying sixteen years until finally moving on in November 1959. No. 62719 is fitted with a G.C.-type tender, received in February 1942, with the early BR emblem. The locomotive was withdrawn in January 1960.

Edinburgh Haymarket 60079
Pictured at the east side of Haymarket shed is Gresley 4-6-2 locomotive no. 60079 *Bayardo*. This engine was one of twenty to be built by the North British locomotive Co. between August and December 1924; *Bayardo* was constructed in October. As LNER no. 2578 the engine was one of the first five A1s to be converted to Class A3, taking place in May 1928 at Darlington. Due to a lapse in communication, Darlington equipped three of the rebuilt A1s with 20-inch-diameter cylinders, when the standard had been set to 19 inches. This was not rectified on *Bayardo* until November 1933. At the time of this photograph, no. 60079 was a Carlisle engine and had been based there since May 1948. *Bayardo* left service in September 1961.

Edinburgh Haymarket 60532

Seen adjacent to the general offices and turntable is Peppercorn Class A2 4-6-2 locomotive no. 60532 *Blue Peter*. The offices were erected at the same time as the shed and housed the shed master's office and the clerical staff. The building also had a store room where lamps and headboards were kept. No. 60532 was built at Doncaster in March 1948 and during September 1949 it was fitted with a double chimney and M.L.S. multi-valve regulator. *Blue Peter* was the last of the Peppercorn A2s to be withdrawn in December 1966 and subsequently went into preservation. The locomotive is currently held by the NELPG and on display at the Barrow Hill Roundhouse awaiting repairs.

Edinburgh Haymarket 76111

The British Railways Standard Class 4 2-6-0 locomotives were built to a design by H. G. Ivatt, based on the LMS Class 4. The example seen here at Haymarket was built in August 1957 at Doncaster Works. Construction of the class started in 1952 concurrently at Horwich Works and Doncaster, and by 1957 they had produced forty-five and seventy respectively. No. 76111 was in the final group of fifteen and all were allocated to the Scottish Region; this locomotive went to Thornton Junction to work passenger services to Edinburgh, Glasgow and Dunfermline. Withdrawal came from Bathgate shed in January 1966, where the engine had been relegated to freight and coal services.

Edinburgh Haymarket 60116

Seen in a dramatic shot at Haymarket shed is Peppercorn Class A1 4-6-2 locomotive no. 60116 *Hal o' the Wynd*. After leaving Doncaster Works in October 1948 the engine was a long-term resident of Heaton shed. It would have been no stranger to Haymarket as the Heaton engines were scheduled on services to Edinburgh. Other duties saw them travel to York, Leeds and Peterborough. No. 60116 was named *Hal o' the Wynd* in May 1951, this being taken from the Sir Walter Scott novel *The Fair Maid of Perth*. The engine saw further service at Tweedmouth and Gateshead and was withdrawn from the latter in June 1965.

Edinburgh Haymarket 60115

Haymarket shed opened in 1894 at a cost of close to £14,000. Consisting of eight open-ended roads, the building was made of brick, while other facilities constructed at the same time included a turntable, coal stage and offices. During the 1930s the facilities were modernised by the addition of a larger turntable and a mechanical coaler. The shed closed to steam in 1963 and was rebuilt specifically to house diesel locomotives in 1965. Class A1 4-6-2 locomotive no. 60115 *Meg Merrilies* entered traffic from Doncaster in September 1948 and was allocated to Gateshead. It was only in service at one other shed, Copley Hill, from November 1960, before withdrawal in November 1962. It was scrapped at Doncaster during the following year.

Edinburgh Dalry Road 57565

LMS 3F Class 0-6-0 locomotive no. 57565 is seen adjacent to the shed at Dalry Road, Edinburgh. The engine was built as part of the Caledonian Railway Class 812 designed by J. F. McIntosh. No. 57565 entered traffic from St Rollox Works in August 1899 as CR no. 827 and was one of seventeen initially built. Seventy-nine more locomotives were erected with construction ceasing in 1909. Ninety-three went to British Railways stock at Nationalisation and all were withdrawn by 1964. No. 57565 left service from Dalry Road, where it had a lengthy allocation, at the end of December 1962. One of the class, no. 57566, survived into preservation.

Edinburgh Dalry Road 55229

0-4-4T locomotive no. 55229 was built in September 1915 at St Rollox Works by the Caledonian Railway as part of the Class 439 designed by J. F. McIntosh. Later, a number of engines were built to a modified design by W. Pickersgill. No. 55229 was withdrawn from Dalry Road in September 1961 and disposal occurred at Inverurie Works in April 1962.

Edinburgh Dalry Road 56312

Dalry Road shed was located just south of Dalry Road Station and was built by the Caledonian Railway. It was of timber construction and opened in 1848 with two dead-end roads. A similar structure was added in 1874 before a four-track shed was added during improvements in 1895. This latter was later rebuilt in 1911. Photographed at the south side of this shed at Dalry Road, next to LMS 'Crab' Class no. 42807, is former Caledonian Railway Class 782 0-6-0T locomotive no. 56312. It was erected at St Rollox Works in May 1907 to a design prepared by J. F. McIntosh. The engine left for Dumfries in November 1960 and was withdrawn from there in May 1962.

Edinburgh Dalry Road 57645

Seen next to Dalry Road's first shed is Class 3F 0-6-0 locomotive no. 57645 built at St Rollox Works in July 1909. The shed was once used as the repair shop, and in the 1960s it was utilised for the maintenance of diesel locomotives. At Grouping the shed was taken over by the LMS. Closure came in October 1965 and the site has been cleared with the West Approach Road now covering both the shed and track areas. No. 57645 was withdrawn from Dalry Road in November 1962.

Perth 54489

Caledonian Railway Class 72 4-4-0 locomotive no. 84 was erected by Armstrong Whitworth & Co. in March 1921. Thirty-two locomotives were built to the designs of W. Pickersgill. Armstrong Whitworth built ten of the class while St Rollox Works added the same number; the remainder came from the North British Locomotive Co. At Grouping the locomotives passed into LMS ownership and no. 84 became LMS no. 14489 and was classified 3P by the company. No. 54489 spent many years allocated to Perth, leaving in December 1961 to be scrapped.

Perth 60027

With the crew taking in the scenery at Perth shed, an opportunity is available to take a portrait shot of Gresley Class A4 Pacific no. 60027 *Merlin*. Built at Doncaster in March 1937 as LNER no. 4486, the locomotive was one of only four A4s to carry the first number in the 1946 renumbering scheme; it was no. 588 from March to May 1946, when it was renumbered 27. While allocated to Haymarket shed (from new until May 1962) it received plaques inscribed with the badge of HMS *Merlin*, and these are visible on the side of the boiler. After leaving Haymarket, two more allocations followed at St Rollox and St Margaret's before withdrawal came in September 1965.

Perth 61243

Seen here at Perth is a Glasgow Eastfield-allocated Thompson Class B1 locomotive. It was built by the North British Locomotive Co. in October 1947 and was named *Sir Harold Mitchell* in December of that year. Visible on the side of the smokebox, below the nameplate, is the steam generator for the electric lighting. Initially alternators on the rear axle were to power the lighting, but these were prone to falling off onto the tracks. From Eastfield, the locomotive would have worked services to Edinburgh and could also find itself in Fort William or Oban in the Highlands. No. 61243's last shed was Ayr and withdrawal from there occurred in May 1964.

Perth 64619

Class J37 0-6-0 locomotive no. 64619 entered service from the North British Locomotive Co.'s Atlas Works in December 1920. It was built as NBR Class B, which gave it a boiler pressure of 165 lbs per square inch. At Grouping the locomotives were classified J37. NBR Class S also became part of the same class, but these locomotives were different in that they had a higher boiler pressure of 175 lbs per square inch. Later, all of the class had their boiler pressure set at 180 lbs per square inch. The locomotive was withdrawn from Dundee Tay Bridge shed in December 1963.

Perth 54500

Many locomotive sheds have existed at Perth, all of varying sizes and designs, and built by many different railway companies. The main shed in operation at the time of this photograph was located to the south of Perth Station and was aptly called Perth South. The first shed was built at the site by the Caledonian Railway in 1854 and was a seven-track dead-end shed. Before the turn of the century, four roads of this shed were extended through the rear of the building and the facilities improved. 4-4-0 locomotive no. 54500, designed by Pickersgill, was built by the NBLC in December 1922 and had a career lasting close to forty years; many of these were spent at Perth. It was condemned in March 1962 and cut up at Arnott Young (Old Kilpatrick) in June 1963.

Perth 72006

In May 1938 the LMS opened a new shed at Perth sited just to the south of the old building. It consisted of eight 'through' tracks with up-to-date facilities. It had been open for twenty-nine years when BR closed it to steam allocations in May 1967; it was then closed to all traffic in October 1969. The site was cleared in the early 1970s and is now occupied by commercial property. British Railways Standard Class 6 4-6-2 locomotive no. 72006 *Clan Mackenzie* was built at Crewe Works in February 1952. It was one of only ten produced in an initial test batch, but due to the clamour for diesel engines no further examples were produced. *Clan Mackenzie* was the last of the class to be withdrawn in May 1966.

Dundee Tay Bridge 64620
Pictured at Dundee Tay Bridge shed next to an unidentified V2 is Class J37 0-6-0 locomotive no. 64620. The shed was located to the west of Dundee Tay Bridge and installed by the North British Railway during the 1890s. The shed was comprised of six tracks, which were through roads, and a slate roof. In this picture the roof has been replaced; this occurred sometime in the late 1950s to early 1960s. The shed closed in May 1967 and was demolished by the end of the decade. No. 64620 left service from Dundee Tay Bridge in April 1967 after a working life of over forty-six years.

Dundee Tay Bridge 64619
Another Class J37 0-6-0 locomotive is seen in sidings near Dundee Tay Bridge shed. No. 64619 was built at the North British Locomotive Company's Atlas Works in December 1920 as part of NBR Class B. The locomotive is attached to a NBR-type tender, which had a capacity of 3,500 gallons and 7 tons of coal. At Grouping, Dundee had eleven of the class available for work, and at Nationalisation this had dropped to nine. By the end of the 1950s it had risen to thirteen, and in 1965 nine were allocated to Dundee Tay Bridge. The end for no. 64619 came in December 1963.

Dundee West 65330

Class J36 0-6-0 locomotive no. 65330 entered service from Cowlairs Works in March 1900. The engine was a member of NBR Class C designed by M. Holmes, which eventually totalled 168; being built between 1888 and 1900. The locomotives were rebuilt by both the NBR and the LNER after Grouping.

Dundee West 69164

Class N15/1 Class 0-6-2T locomotive no. 69164 was built by the North British Locomotive Co. at their Queen's Park Works in may 1913. The engine had a coal capacity of 4 tons and could hold 1,586 gallons of water. It has BR black livery with red and cream lining, which was normally reserved for passenger locomotives. After a spell at Dunfermline the engine arrived at Dundee Tay Bridge in August 1958, but lasted less than a year; it was withdrawn in April 1959.

Dundee West 62426
Cowlairs Works built NBR Class J 4-4-0 no. 417 *Cuddie Headrigg* in July 1914 to the design of William Reid. A total of forty-three engines were completed with different boilers; saturated and superheated. At Grouping the locomotives were split by the LNER into Classes D29 and D30. NBR no. 417 became LNER no. 9417 and classified D30/2; the two prototypes for the superheated engines were classified D30/1. The D30/2 locomotives were slightly modified from the prototypes in having increased superheater elements and reduced small boiler tubes. They also had two inches added to the diameter of the piston valves, making them ten inches. As BR no. 62426, withdrawal from Stirling came in June 1960.

Dundee West 62470
Pictured at Dundee West is Class D34 4-4-0 locomotive no. 62470 *Glen Roy*, which was one of the first five of the class to be built at Cowlairs Works in September 1913. Ten were built in 1913 with two types of superheater. Five, including no. 62470, had the Robinson type, while the remainder were fitted with Schmidt's. The engines with the Schmidt superheater were later fitted with those of Robinson's, and this became standard for other locomotives built in the class. No. 62470 was withdrawn in May 1959 and one of the class, no. 62469 *Glen Douglas,* has been preserved.

Forfar 55209

Forfar's first shed was constructed by the Arbroath & Forfar Railway in 1839. Originally the track was a larger gauge, being 5 feet 6 inches, than that which became standard. This was changed in 1846 and the shed closed in 1850 to be replaced by a more substantial building erected by the CR. LMS Class 2P-H 0-4-4T locomotive no. 55209, built at St Rollox Works in April 1911, entered service as CR no. 154, later becoming LMS no. 15209. The locomotive was withdrawn in September 1961.

Forfar 54467

Former Caledonian Railway Class 113, 4-4-0 locomotive no. 54467, was built by the North British Locomotive Co. in March 1916, one of only sixteen examples ever produced. CR Class 113 later became LMS Class 3P-G. The four-track shed seen behind the locomotive was built by the Caledonian Railway in 1899, replacing a structure built by the company in 1850. This closed to steam in July 1964 and went into private use. No. 54467 was allocated to Perth at the time of this photograph, and was withdrawn from there in October 1959.

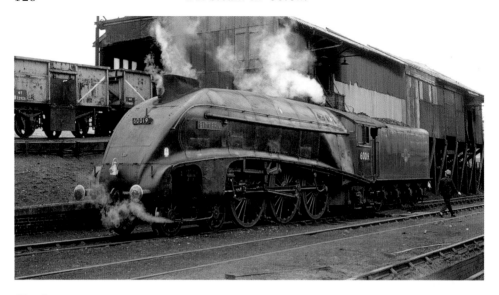

Aberdeen 60019
Taking on coal at Aberdeen Ferryhill shed is Gresley Class A4 4-6-2 locomotive no. 60019 *Bittern*.
The coaling stage was installed around 1908 during modifications to the original shed and site.
The engine entered service in December 1937 and was allocated to Heaton. This was followed by a
move to Gateshead and a month at St Margaret's before joining the other banished A4s at Aberdeen
in November 1963. Fourteen of the class were allocated to Aberdeen before withdrawal and some
survived longer than others; eight were left in 1965, working Aberdeen to Glasgow services. *Bittern*
was one of the last two to be withdrawn in September 1966, and it was subsequently preserved.

Aberdeen Kittybrewster 65297
Seen at Kittybrewster shed, Aberdeen, is Class J36 0-6-0 locomotive no. 65297. The engine was
built by Cowlairs Works in July 1897 and was later rebuilt by the NBR in June 1922. When
built, the locomotive employed Westinghouse brakes and at Grouping also used vacuum brakes.
However, the locomotive had its Westinghouse equipment removed and from then on used steam
and vacuum braking. In its later years the locomotive was allocated to Kittybrewster, arriving from
Keith in April 1959; it transferred to Ferryhill in July 1961. Several other moves followed before it
left service in January 1966.

Bibliography

Batty, Stephen R. *Rail Centres: Doncaster*, 2007

Bolger, Paul *BR Steam Motive Power Depots – North Eastern Region*, 2009

Bolger, Paul. *BR Steam Motive Power Depots – Scottish Region*. 2009.

Buck, Martin and Mark Rawlinson *Line by Line: The East Coast Main Line Kings Cross to Edinburgh*, 2002

Butt, R. V. J. *The Directory of Railway Stations*, 1995

Clough, David N. *British Rail Standard Diesels of the 1960s*, 2009

Fawcett, Bill *A History of North Eastern Railway Architecture Volume Two: A Mature Art*, 2003

Griffiths, Roger and John Hooper *Great Northern Railway Engine Sheds Volume 1: Southern Area*, 2001

Griffiths, Roger and John Hooper *Great Northern Railway Engine Sheds Volume 2: The Lincolnshire Loop, Nottinghamshire and Derbyshire*, 1996

Griffiths, Roger and John Hooper, *Great Northern Railway Engine Sheds Volume 3: Yorkshire and Lancashire*, 2000

Griffiths, Roger and Paul Smith, *The Directory of British Engine Sheds and Principle Locomotive Servicing Points: 1*, 1999

Griffiths, Roger and Paul Smith, *The Directory of British Engine Sheds and Principle Locomotive Servicing Points: 2*, 2000

Grindlay, Jim *British Railways Steam Locomotive Allocations 1948-1968: Part Three London Midland and Scottish Regions 40001-58937*, 2008

Hoole, Ken *Rail Centres: Newcastle*, 1986

Hoole, Ken *North Eastern Locomotive Sheds*, 1972

Hoole, Ken *Rail Centres: York*, 1983

Hoole, Ken *The East Coast Main Line Since 1925*, 1977

Hooper, J. *The WD Austerity 2-8-0: The BR Record*, 2010

Knox, Harry *Haymarket Motive Power Depot, Edinburgh: A History of the depot, its Works and Locomotives 1842-2010*, 2011

Larkin, Edgar *An Illustrated History of British Railways' Workshops*, 2007

Locomotives Illustrated No. 4: Peppercorn Pacifics

Locomotives Illustrated No. 9: The V2s

Locomotives Illustrated No. 10: BR Standard Pacifics

Locomotives Illustrated No. 20: Gresley Eight-Coupled Locomotives

Locomotives Illustrated No. 21: BR Standard Tank Locomotives

Locomotives Illustrated No. 25: Gresley 'A1'/'A3' Pacifics

Locomotives Illustrated No. 30: The B1 4-6-0s

Locomotives Illustrated No. 38: The LNER 'A4' Pacifics, June-August 1984

Locomotives Illustrated No. 46: The Thompson Pacifics, February-March 1986

Locomotives Illustrated No. 103: The LMS 'Royal Scot' 4-6-0s, September/October 1995

Marshall, Peter *The Railways of Dundee*, 1996

Morrison, Brian *The Power of the A4's*, n.d.

Mullay, A. J. *Rail Centres: Edinburgh*, 1991

Penney, Derek *LNER Pacifics in Colour*, 1997

Pike M.B.E., S. N. *Mile by Mile on the LNER: Kings Cross Edition*, 1951

Quick, Michael *Railway Passenger Stations in Great Britain: A Chronology*, 2009

RCTS *Locomotives of the LNER: Part 1 Preliminary Survey*, 1963

RCTS *Locomotives of the LNER: Part 2A Tender Engines – Classes A1 to A10*, 1978

RCTS *Locomotives of the LNER: Part 2B Tender Engines – Classes B1 to B19*, 1975

RCTS *Locomotives of the LNER: Part 3A Tender Engines – Classes C1 to C11*, 1979

RCTS *Locomotives of the LNER: Part 3B Tender Engines – Classes D1 to 12*, 1980

RCTS *Locomotives of the LNER: Part 3C Tender Engines – Classes D13 to D24*, 1981

RCTS *Locomotives of the LNER: Part 4 Tender Engines – Classes D25 to E7*, 1968

RCTS *Locomotives of the LNER: Part 5 Tender Engines – Classes J1 to J37*, 1984

RCTS *Locomotives of the LNER: Part 6A Tender Engines – Classes J38 to K5*, 1982

RCTS *Locomotives of the LNER: Part 6B Tender Engines – Classes O1 to P2*, 1991

RCTS *Locomotives of the LNER: Part 6C Tender Engines – Classes Q1 to Y10*, 1984

RCTS *Locomotives of the LNER: Part 7 Tank Engines – Classes A5 to H2*, 1991

RCTS *Locomotives of the LNER: Part 8A Tank Engines – Classes J50 to J70*, 1970

RCTS *Locomotives of the LNER: Part 8B Tank Engines – Class J71 to J94*, 1971

RCTS *Locomotives of the LNER: Part 9A Tank Engines – Classes L1 to N19*, 1977

RCTS *Locomotives of the LNER: Part 9B Tank Engines – Classes Q1 to Z5*, 1977

RCTS *Locomotives of the LNER: Part 10A Departmental Stock, Locomotive Sheds, Boiler and Tender Numbering*, 1991

RCTS *British Railways Standard Steam Locomotives Volume 1: Background to Standardisation and the Pacific Classes*, 1994

RCTS *British Railways Standard Steam Locomotives Volume 2: The 4-6-0 and 2-6-0 Classes*, 2003

RCTS *British Railways Standard Steam Locomotives Volume 4: The 9F 2-10-0 Class*, 2008

The Railways of Aberdeen: 150 Years of History, 2000

Walmsley, Tony *Shed by Shed Part Two: Eastern*, 2010

Waszak, P. *Rail Centres: Peterborough*, 2005

Whiteley, J. S. and G. W. Morrison *The Power of the A1's, A2's and A3's*, 1982

Yeadon, W. B. *Yeadon's Register of LNER Locomotives Volume One: Gresley A1 and A3 Classes*, 2001

Yeadon, W. B. *Yeadon's Register of LNER Locomotives Volume Two: Gresley A4 and W1 Classes*, 2001

Yeadon, W. B. *Yeadon's Register of LNER Locomotives Volume Three: Raven, Thompson and Peppercorn Pacifics*, 2001

Yeadon, W. B. *Yeadon's Register of LNER Locomotives Volume Four: Gresley V2 and V4 Classes*, 2001

Yeadon, W. B. *Yeadon's Register of LNER Locomotives Volume Six: Thompson B1 Class*, 2001

Yeadon, W. B. *Yeadon's Register of LNER Locomotives Volume Nine: Gresley 8-Coupled Engines Classes O1, O2, P1, P2 and U1*, 1995